D0031206

THE POETRY LESSON

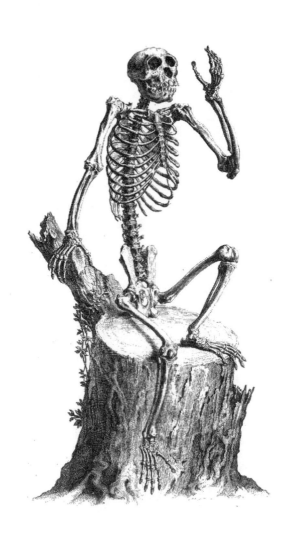

THE POETRY LESSON

Andrei CODRESCU

PRINCETON UNIVERSITY PRESS
Princeton & Oxford

Published by Princeton University Press,
41 William Street, Princeton, New Jersey 08540
In the United Kingdom: Princeton University Press,
6 Oxford Street, Woodstock, Oxfordshire OX20 1TW
press.princeton.edu

Library of Congress Cataloging-in-Publication Data

Codrescu, Andrei, 1946–
The poetry lesson / Andrei Codrescu.
p. cm.
ISBN 978-0-691-14724-6 (cloth : alk. paper)
I. Title.
PS3553.O3P64 2010
813'.54—dc22
2010006053

British Library Cataloging-in-Publication Data is available

This book has been composed in
Printed on acid-free paper. ∞
Printed in the United States of America
10 9 8 7 6 5 4 3 2 1

THE POETRY LESSON

THE DAY THE UNIVERSITY TESTED ITS TEXT-MESSAGE ALERT to every cell phone on campus, I assigned epitaphs to my "Introduction to Poetry Writing" class.

"Every morning when you get up, write an epitaph!" I watched them scribble something. "That's good," I encouraged them, "start right away!," though I knew that what they were scribbling were not epitaphs, but "every morning when you get up write an epi . . . epipi . . . epi . . . "

"And while you're at it, turn off your cell phones!" I always say this the first class of the semester, but I didn't realize that now they would be unable to receive the text-message alert test. If a real wacko wired to a bomb tried shooting his way to fame inside this very door, we'd have been unwarned. I consoled myself with the fact that the Virginia Tech wacko who had killed fellow students had been *enrolled* in poetry class. If there was a wacko, he could be in *my* class, writing his epitaph.

"An epitaph a day is like an apple a day, but the opposite, actually, because an apple a day keeps the doctor away, but an epitaph is ready if you happen to die that day. The apple part is *rhymed poetry*, the dying part is *blank verse*."

I gave them examples of famous epitaphs, by *blank verse poets* like Ted Berrigan, "See you later," and "Have a nice day," and by *rhyming poets*, such as John Keats, who only wrote part of his own epitaph, either because he died too young, or because his executors found it too terse: "This grave contains all that was mortal of a young English poet who on his death bed in the bitterness of his heart at the malicious power of his enemies desired these words to be engraven on his tomb stone: 'Here lies One Whose Name was writ in Water,'" "which doesn't rhyme," I explained, "and not only doesn't it rhyme, but the poet's name is *entirely* missing. In this regard, at least, they respected his wish even as they choked it in prose."

"It's a good thing that when I visited the grave of John Keats in Rome in the Protestant cemetery where he is buried next to Gregory Corso, a cat who lives in the cemetery stole the *panino* with mortadella from my jacket pocket and made off with it in the direction of a pyramid built CE by a Roman senator during one of the periodic Egyptian crazes of the Romans. Too bad too, because I didn't have any money and I'd gotten the sandwich from a nun in a charity-dispensing convent. Behind the grave of John Keats grows a lyre-shaped tree that is obviously pruned carefully, though the cemetery itself, at the time of my visit, was in a state of neglect. Next to John Keats is buried his friend Joseph Severn, whose epitaph notes that he is the friend of John Keats, the poet buried next to him. So that even though John Keats's *name* is missing *from his own grave*, he is made present by his dead friend next to him, which is *a kind of rhyme*. What does this tell us?"

A skinny mop-styled redhead girl fingering what looked like a worry bead that was actually the earbud of her iPod said: "That if you don't write your epigram you might have to rely on your friends?"

"Precisely. I now assign you in addition to an *epitaph* an

epigram. For this class, you must also write an *epigram* every day. An epigram is a very short poem with a *clever twist* at the end that shows off your *wit.* For example, '*In my next life I will make a lot of croaking noises / but I will live a long time / because in my next life / I will be a gold frog / like the one that sits on your desk, father.*' This is an epigram I made up in the style of the *Roman poet Lucian.* Now, if I was in a hurry, I might combine my assignments into an *epitogram,* which is an *epitaph plus an epigram,* something like, '*I am a gold frog in this life / and I will leap at you / from behind this tombstone / when you are finished reading.*' And then I would jump out and scare the shit out of the poor pilgrim to my grave, who happens to be an executive for a U.S. insurance company with a penchant for poetry, like *Wallace Stevens,* who is vacationing by visiting the graves of *important poets* around the world. Can you identify the *wit* in this epitogram?"

A boy with a crewcut spoke from the back: "The price of gold, like, from the time the poet died and the time when the business guy was visiting?"

"Very *astute.* The business guy maybe was amazed by how cheap gold used to be when those poets lived and how much it was now, and he couldn't feel his amazement properly until he saw the poets' graves. That was one weird cat, right, but I'm not sure *witty* is the word for him. Before going to visit *John Keats,* he visited the following poets: *Walt Whitman* in Camden, New Jersey, *Emily Dickinson* in Amherst, Massachusetts, *Edgar Allan Poe* in Baltimore, Maryland, *Tristan Tzara* at the Montparnasse cemetery in Paris, France, *Guillaume Apollinaire* in the Père Lachaise cemetery in Paris, France, where he also stopped briefly to say hello to *Jim Morrison.* He saw *George Bacovia* in Bacău, Romania, *Boris Pasternak* in Moscow, Russia, before his tomb was desecrated by vandals in 2006, and *César Vallejo* in Mont-rouge, the communist cemetery in Paris, France."

I looked around the class to see if maybe Jim Morrison elicited recognition. A soft stirring. Nothing much.

"What does this *say* about this man?"

"That he's rich?" tried the future jokester-in-chief of the class, a square-shouldered boy named Bennigan. Class laughed. "And that there are a lot of *poets* buried in Paris, France?" Another boy slapped him five. Villanelles for you, Bennigan.

"Yes, poets are buried in Paris to make it easier for tourists. Poets are one big family. Anyway, at each grave this man took pictures. A couple of years later when he was found shot dead in the small apartment he kept secretly in lower Manhattan, the police detective in charge of the case, Detective Emma Flores, took pictures of these photographs of the poets' graves, framed along the walls. She believed that there was a connection. Frustrated by what she believed was her *ignorance of poetry*, she enrolled at the New School and took a beginner class in Writing Poetry with *poet and teacher Sharon Mesmer*. You would be right to ask, 'Did she solve the case?'"

Nobody said anything.

"The answer is no. Professor Mesmer's method of writing poetry at that time, in the early years of the twenty-first century, consisted of entering a number of blog postings into a Googlator, a program that mixes up words in *strange combinations* and returns them to you in *novel forms*."

"I thought that this was supposed to be a *poetry* class," said a disaffected voice from the back, with hair hanging over the mouth, a voice, I instantly thought, destined for greatness. It exuded intelligence from under all that hair, like an animal's breath on a frosty morning.

"You must speak clearly in this class. You must *enunciate*. What did you say?"

"There is a *novel writing* class," he enunciated.

"Yes, you could have taken that and yes, it's true, there are *novel forms* in which to write *novels*, but when I speak of *novel forms*, I generally mean them to apply to *poetry* because *poetry generates novel forms more quickly and more easily than novels*, which are long. What is your name?"

"Matthew Borden."

Matthew Borden, as I immediately found out by googling his family tree on my desktop computer, was the grandchild of the founder of the famous milk empire. For many years I'd seen his gleaming family trucks hurtling milk on the highways.

"Matt, your family business is pretty poetic. Do they approve of your interest in poetry?" I had no idea if Matthew was interested in poetry—maybe he was in it just for his English requirement—but I saw bursting udders on frosty mornings being milked by 4-H beauty queens and I became momentarily lost. I knew that machines did the milking now, and then there were details like penned animals and hormones, but there you have it. Poetry.

Matt said, "My side of the family is pretty artistic. We have a farm of super-cows, more like a showcase for kids. The animals live in heated stalls that are better than some public housing. Their names and genetic history are carved on wood over each stall. Some of them even have small televisions for entertainment. The best of them eat apples that are hand-fed to them by *German-speaking Wisconsin high school girls*."

He couldn't have enunciated more clearly. The face that was hidden before came out of its hairy nest, looking consumptive. He was not a mumbler, but had widespread ec-

5

zema, covering both cheeks. His eyes flashed. "There are some poets in the Borden family!"

"Lizzie?" asked Bennigan.

Matt Borden grinned. "My grandmother was a personal friend of Queen Marie of Romania. They exchanged *poetry*."

I had to admit it. I'd been out-googled. This kid knew not only that I was from Romania, but that Queen Marie, his grandmother's friend, wrote verses in the 1920s and made many friends in America, including a lumber baron in Washington in whose castle she spent the night, leaving in the morning for the next stop on her triumphal train tour. The baron transformed the castle into a museum dedicated to her memory. It was the most touching one-night stand in the history of poetry.

I asked him if he possesssed any of his grandmother's poems and whether he might read some in class.

Matt Borden shook his head sadly. "Her poetry was buried with her in the grave in North Dakota. She left in her will that all her books had to be buried in bookcases around her tomb. She only published one book and she has that with her inside the sculpture."

"A *catafalque*?"

"Yeah, well, it's a story. The family had to import a French sculptor, originally she wanted Rodin, but he was already dead, to make a life-size bronze of Diana the Huntress in my grandma's likeness. She was buried standing inside of it . . ."

I was astonished, and the class was nervously fingering earbuds, doodling in their open notebooks, shifting in their seats, etc. I didn't blame them. It was a wacky story. I knew it was true because Queen Marie'd been a flapper, friend of Isadora Duncan and Rodin, among others. If the Queen and

6

the Borden woman had palled about in Paris in the 1920s, they'd have surely posed naked before Rodin at one time or another.

"And the statue of Diana, the grave, stands in the family cemetery bearing a poetic inscription? What does it say?"

"Well, actually, no. Grandma died in the Eighties when they removed a bunch of intercontinental ballistic missiles from the Dakotas because of the SALT Treaty, and she bought a decommissioned nuclear silo. It's thirty stories deep. She stands in the center of what used to be the control room on the bottom."

I didn't quite understand. If she was buried in the family cemetery, how could she be resting in a decommissioned silo ... unless ...?

Matt guessed my unspoken question. "Yeah. She also left in her will that the family cemetery had to be moved into the silo. Now we are all on different levels, buried into the walls between bookshelves. The place is pretty big, there is a lot more room. All of us have spaces in there already, me too, with my birthdate engraved, because I'm not dead."

"Not yet!" said Bennigan. Nobody laughed. He knew that no matter how funny he was going to be in the future, he would not elicit such deeply emotional scent from a room full of people, such girlish sweat, such creepy-crawly terror in the armpits ... Magnificent. The classroom was like a stall filled with excited mammals. They gave off pheromones. Terror. Desire. Matt Borden was Lord Byron.

"Matt, I'm not quite getting the picture, would you very much mind coming up here and drawing this unusual structure on the blackboard?"

"No problem." Looking bored, he strolled to the blackboard. He was overweight and sloppy, his jeans hung low and the plaid flannel shirt hung out of them in the back. He took his time, chalk in hand, eyes half-closed. Then he drew. The silo-cemetery looked like this:

Matt strolled back. He had the bored air of someone who

could do anything he might be asked, like solve a quantum equation, but he only did it as a personal favor. He himself was bored by all earthly things because he knew them well, though he knew that many other people, for reasons he didn't quite understand, didn't.

"And the *epitaph*? What is written on her sculpture-grave?" I was trying to get back to teaching *poetry* proper, which is what they paid me for.

"There are no *words*. She's Diana the Huntress, bronze by Louis Kleppner, Rodin imitator."

There are no words. More dreadful things were never spoken on the cold hillside. Not in Intro to Poetry Writing, anyway.

I took the deep breath customary in this sort of situation, unique as it was. Taking a deep breath can, if done right, take a thing out of uniqueness and place it in a genus. Matt's was a *family* story.

I got up and turned to the blackboard. "I'm going to write down for you *the tools of poetry*. Take note. By next week, you must have eight of them. There are two that have a purpose I'm not going to reveal to you until midterm." I wrote:

THE TOOLS OF POETRY

1. A goatskin notebook for writing down dreams
2. Mont Blanc fountain pen (extra credit if it belonged to Mme Blavatsky)
3. A Chinese coin or a stone in your pocket for rubbing
4. Frequenting places where you can overhear things
5. Tiny recorders, spyglasses, microscopic listening devices
6. A little man at the back of your head
7. The Ghost-Companion

8. Susceptibility to hypnosis
9. Large sheets of homemade paper, a stack a foot thick
10. A subscription to cable TV

"To number five, there is an exception," I said. "You cannot record anything said in this class because I don't want to go to prison for things I've said. Intro to Poetry Writing is like the confessional. Things said here are like things only your priest or your therapist is allowed to hear. Nobody in this class is permitted to repeat anything anybody in this class said or wrote. The reason for your goatskin notebook is so you can write an oath in blood in it, swearing never to whisper a word of what we say here."

I looked around. "Only kidding," I added, seeing some sincerely frightened faces, "there is no blood oath. But with the Internet these days it's hard to keep things discreet. I realize that this is not why you're here, that some of you may even want to be famous so that everybody in the world can read your poetry, but you must hold your horses until Poetry Writing 4007, which comes after Intro 2007, and is being taught by a terrible poet and execrable human being, even though he's a colleague of mine."

I waited out the chuckles, and continued. "The goatskin notebook is for you to write your dreams in. Every day without fail you must write down what you dreamt even if you haven't slept in weeks, which is what I did when I was your age. In addition to dreams you must write down *poetic ideas*, which are these thoughts that come to you when you least expect them. Until now, you probably thought of these kinds of sudden thoughts as annoying, like involuntary twitches or muscle spasms, but they are actually *poetic ideas*. You are no longer allowed to dismiss them. You must write them down in your goatskin notebook. Also in your goatskin notebook you must jot down *things that you are not supposed to hear*. Once you start frequenting places where you can overhear things, you must listen for *things that you are not supposed to hear*, even if, as it often happens, you *mishear* them. *Mishearing* is one of the *muses of poetry*. There are *ten muses of poetry*."

I stood up and wrote on the blackboard, to the left of the Borden family cemetery:

THE TEN MUSES OF POETRY
1. Mishearing
2. Misunderstanding
3. Mistranslating
4. Mismanaging
5. Mislaying
6. Misreading
7. Misappropriating cliches
8. Misplacing objects belonging to roommates or lovers
9. Misguided thoughts at inappropriate times, funerals, etc.
10. Mississippi (the river)

"Are we clear on this? Be clear on this because all of it is part of your next week's assignment. The *epitogram* is a permanent assignment, an everyday thing, but in addition you'll get a *special* assignment every week. You have to forgive my handwriting, I was taught cursive in Europe by a German-trained teacher. 'Madame Blavatsky' is spelled with a 'y' at the end. Number two of your rules is to help place you within the family of poets. Every poet worth his or her salt, and, trust me, this is the only reward we get for the hard work we do, and in this sense we are still one with the ancient Romans who valued salt above all else, as does, I'm sure, the Borden family, whose cows, no matter what their level of culture, still require their salt licks, every salty poet, then, had a good fountain pen. The best of all fountain pens is the Mont Blanc, but it's terribly expensive because of its gold nib and reputation. A Mont Blanc that had belonged to Madame Blavatsky would be the instrument through which the disembodied voices of angels and demons would have traveled into the many volumes of books dictated to her by these otherworldly entities. In other words, you would be possessing an angelic instrument that, should it turn up on eBay, would fetch easily one to three hundred thousand dollars. Your extra credit for owning such a pen would amount to one fourth of your final grade. You wouldn't have one of *these*, Matthew?"

"We do, actually, but it's been buried with grandma."

"Let me explain number six in the context of Madame Blavatsky's fountain pen, before I get to number seven, which is the most important part of your assignment. Are we being funny, Mr. Borden? No? Good. Number six, *a little man at the back of your head*, was called that by *the poet Ted Berrigan*, in an interview. He meant, I believe, that there is a little man at the back of every poet's head who dictates things to the poet. The *poet Ted Berrigan* lived in chauvinistic days, in the Sixties of the last century. A decade later, he might have said *the little man/woman at the back of your head*, and a few months later *the little person at the back of your head*, and not long after that, *the person at the back of your head*, and maybe even later, in like 1981, he might have said just *a voice at the back of your head*, 'person' having meanwhile gone the way of 'man' and 'man/woman' and 'little man/woman,' discredited by poets who no longer believed in 'persons,' and not long after that, he might not have said 'voice,' the idea of 'voice', of 'having a voice' having been hurled down the garbage chute of poetry, to be soon followed by 'the back of,' a phrase implying something hierarchical and unsavory. He would have been left only with the word 'head,' which means so many things he'd have preferred to not speak at all. Which for *the poet Ted Berrigan* would have been impossible. On the other hand, *the poet Ted Berrigan* wouldn't have paid the slightest attention to those shifts because when he discovered and named *a little man at the back of your head*, he had already used many terrific things that the little man had said, and once these things were written down, no revisionism could erase them. So I'm using number six, *a little man at the back of your head*, as a historical personage, like somebody out of Shakespeare, who whispers poetry to you and answers the questions you didn't know you had. Let me amend that: the *little man at the back of your head* answers questions you don't know the answer to, rather than asking the questions himself, though he's not above it. When you write your next week's assignment, use *whatever the little man at the back of your head says*, no matter how nonsensical, because in combination with number two and number seven, you might just be lucky enough to land a poem. If you employ, that is, *the ten muses of poetry.*"

I noticed that they had stopped taking notes. Students! Accursèd youth!

"I will now explain number seven, the most important part of your assignment, the Ghost-Companion. Please let me see your *Millennium* textbook."

Eager hands lifted the textbook in the air: *Poems for the Millennium, Volume Two*, edited by Jerome Rothenberg and Pierre Joris. Some of them used two hands—it was a big book.

"I meant you to use both volumes for textbooks, but Volume One is out of print. I assigned instead, *World Poetry of the Stone and Bronze Ages*, an anthology that, together with *Poems for the Millennium, Volume Two*, should introduce you sufficiently to the exceedingly difficult but mind-numbingly simple art of composing poesy. In any case, here is how we will proceed."

I opened the manila folder on which I'd written "Intro to Poetry Writing," and took out the class roster. These were their names. I read them out loud:

Adams, Hillary
Bennigan, Zaccariah, "Zed"
Borden, Matthew, "Matt"
Chamoix, Chloe
Ferris, John, "Jack"
Garland, Beatrice, "Betty"
Helmick, Gertrude, "Trudy"
Jacob, Jason, "JJ"
Klein, Letitia, "Red"
Minneaux, Sylvia, "Sylvie"
Rios, Carlos, "Señor C"
Saunders, Rebecca
Washington, Anita

I then opened *Poems for the Millennium, Volume Two* to the index.

"Miss Adams, Hillary." I cast about until I noted one finger raised at right-ear height by a small person dressed in a loose ROTC uniform. I remembered that there was a war going on, and I felt suddenly lousy. A young person like that, paying her college tuition by enlisting, could be sent to Iraq by next class and be killed before she could complete her assignment. Then I felt nauseous. Most of my ideas about poetry had been forged during another war, the war in Vietnam. Most of my ideas were antiwar, which is why they took the aggressive shape they took. My pedagogy was guerrilla warfare against war! I wasn't sure if teaching this young woman poetry was right or wrong. Suppose that she was going to fulfill all her assignments before she was killed! What then? If she fulfilled all her assignments she'd become as antiwar as I was, but it wouldn't be so easy for her to shed the uniform and skip the country like many people had in my youth. For one thing, she would be barely aware that she was drinking antiwar poison by fulfilling her assignments, and for another, she might become perfectly aware of it around, let's say, midterm, and kill *me*. Of course, she could always drop out before resorting to *that*. We could even make a deal. She could come to my office during office hours and denounce my tactics, whereupon I would make her a deal: if you drop out now I'll give you a passing grade! And by the way, how do you look under that ill-fitting camouflage? Perky, I bet.

"Hillary, I am going to give you a Ghost-Companion. This is a poet, dead or alive, from this big poetry book, whose last name begins with the same letter as yours. This is a poet that you will study all semester, read deeply, understand well, google till you're satisfied, and call on when you feel some difficulty. *Any* difficulty. Your Ghost-Companion will be a great and generous soul, who will come to your aid not just for your assignments, but also in other situations that neither you nor I can now imagine. If she or he is dead, you will reach him or her by Telepathic Mail, T-mail. If she or he is alive you can call her on the phone, or send an e-mail to his agent, or write a letter to the editor of the *New York Times Book Review*, protesting the careless reviewer who saw *so little* of your G-C's last book's grandeur. If your Ghost-Companion is still alive, you will earn his or her eternal gratitude, possibly a place at his or her table or bed, and a surefire letter of recommendation and a blurb."

I paused significantly, but she stayed with me. She lowered her finger, though. A good sign. I ran my eyes down the As. Adonis, Akhmatova, Albiach, Andrews, Antin, Appel, Armantrout, Artaud, Artmann, Ashbery. Some dead, some alive.

"I give you a choice, Hillary. Anna Akhmatova, a Russian poet from the early twentieth century who barely escaped being killed by communists and was not allowed to publish for twenty years, or Rae Armantrout, born in 1947, who published many books and belongs to a group called the Language poets. This 'language poetry' is something I will explain later, but suffice it to say that 'language' poets claim to be influenced by the Russian poets of Akhmatova's generation. How and in what way I'll clarify later, but you have to choose now, sight unseen."

Without much deliberation, Hillary said, "I'll take the dead Russian."

I don't know why, but I was gratified. Rae Armantrout is wonderful and if I'd had another A in class I'd have gladly handed her over, but I didn't. Next time.

"Any questions you might have, Hillary, just e-mail me. And if you're uncomfortable with Anna Akhmatova, who was a pretty wild woman from what I've read, don't hesitate to trade her in. She wasn't just wild, she suffered in terrible ways. You could always take Rae if hunger, disease, communism, Russia, spiritual hurt, and nymphomania are not your cup of tea."

"I can take it," my soldier said.

I'm a softie.

But not all that soft. I had an idea.

I called for a "cigarette break." This must have sounded as quaint to them as someone calling the latest iTunes™ release an "album." Few if any of them smoked. A few years ago they'd have stepped on each other to rush outside, fiddling with their lighters the whole time. Years ago we'd have all smoked in class. Some of these basement classrooms were as hazy as commie print shops before the Russian Revolution. Of course, back then every poet was a revolutionary troublemaker and doomed soul, in accordance with the zeitgeist. One of them, a chunky boy inflamed by the Beats, claimed a spot in front of the Student Union, where he shouted his masterwork, "I Want a Girl with Cocksucker Lips," at future petroleum engineeers and accounting majors. His only competition was the preaching couple with the baby who took turns haranguing the crowd. The woman held the baby while the man thundered against fornication, masturbation, and sodomy, and then it was his turn to hold the baby, while his wife began, in a quiet voice, to describe her pre-Christian life that included oral sex with five fraternity boys behind a Physics building stairway one satanic night. She described in detail the penises that she'd fondled and engorged, and the boys who masturbated waiting their turn. She confessed to feeling degraded, yet thrilled sufficiently by Satan to fondle herself, and she even remembered the black satin panties she wore. The preaching couple acquired an appreciative audience, particularly attentive to the poetic detail that grew increasingly more vivid: they began by applauding, then cheering and, as the audience grew larger, jostling for a place at the front. My poor poetry student, soon bereft of his fans, took to shouting louder and louder, but only a faint "cocksucker" made it now and then through the preachers' clamoring mob. One day his voice gave out, he dropped out of school, and the Christians had the whole stage. Complaints to the police, originally occasioned by the poet's foul language, ceased completely, leading the University to dub the square of cement in front of the Student Union "Free Speech Alley." After that, the only free speech practiced there was Christian and apocalyptic, and when the couple moved away, the crowd vanished as well. The place is now an island for the occasional mutterer whose Bible thumping arrests no one.

Fickle art! After the Free Speech Island became deserted, there was no longer any street theater on campus or in the city, and, most likely, anywhere else in America. The poets went indoors like sheep to compete for time with standup comedians. I headed for my own performance space: the office. A forlorn sanctum: I kept few office hours.

The hallway was lined with old computers, the school having just purchased sleek new models. Old computers were on perennial display here, rising from the floor two thirds of the way up to the ceiling, unmoved by the invisible janitorial staff until a new wave of obsolete machines poured out. When I first started teaching I was dreaming of an electric typewriter, an IBM with a "ball," a dream that came true when the English Department office retired theirs in favor of the first PC, an ugly thing with 36 kilobytes of memory. I sat in front of that IBM "Selectric" with a "ball," more upright than I ever had in years of slouching over a notebook in coffeehouses, and when I started tapping I was Mayakovsky addressing the masses through the megaphone of history. Another Russian poet who didn't fare so well in the end. Killed himself as a gift to Lenin.

I figured that the three-hour class had lasted an hour, but it was a pure guess because sometime during the last five years, the clock in the hall had disappeared. It had never been right anyway, its inaccuracies ranging wildly from fifteen minutes to six or seven hours. The old thing was amusing, if nothing else, because I had a watch in those days. I loved tapping my watch and pointing out the hallway clock to some passing student. "Time, eh?" But sometime between the end of the millennium and the beginning of the new century, I ceased wearing my watch. The leather band got sweaty and made my wrist smell like Roquefort. I also discovered that I had an allergy to metals, a severe allergy that could cause a rash all over my body, starting either from my belt buckle or my watch. I gave up wearing belts with metal buckles and gave up the watch. I started using my cell phone to tell time. It wasn't the easiest thing. It was comparable, I suppose, to a pocket watch. I had to take it out of my pocket, flip it open to wake it up, close it, then quickly read the time on its small screen, before it went dark again. I had faith in the cell phone because time, as I understood it, was set by my provider (I almost said "the phone company"), an infallible entity surely connected to the atomic clock at Greenwich. Then, just as they brought in the latest wave of computers, the strangest thing happened: the time on my cell phone became consistently *wrong*. Not by a lot, at first. Ten minutes at most, but ten minutes is huge in the life of a teacher, who must be punctual. In a short time, its accuracy declined severely. It refused to recognize Daylight Savings Time. It failed to return to its time zone after I'd gone into another, East or West. In addition, the metal the phone was made from unleashed my rash after being held to my ear for even the shortest conversation. Laura found a leather case that covered most of the metal parts, and that worked OK as long as I didn't talk too long or try to tell time on it. She also wrapped the metal portion of my eyeglasses in scotch tape so that no part of my body could now come in touch with metal. I had become a sort of involuntary vegetarian, a Stone Age person who had only a vague idea of time. Metals hadn't yet been invented.

I unlocked the office door, flipped on the light switch, and beheld my ageless den. Shelves piled high with thousands of unsold copies of my literary journal (before it became an Internet publication in 1996); hundreds of poetry books gone undonated to the University's yearly book sale; thousands of unopened manila envelopes containing the hopes of generations of poets; file cabinets overstuffed with folders and diskettes (remember "diskettes"? How about "floppy disks"?) piled high with more folders and envelopes and books; the guts of successive generations of reproductive technology. No, not the genetic kind. Back before cloning, reproduction was generally intended to mean "making copies." Our revolutionary slogan, "Seize the Means of Reproduction," was not a call to confiscate women's wombs or fertilized eggs, but was aimed at the publishing establishment. We were what used to be called a "small" or "alternative" press, as opposed to the corporate book providers in New York, unaware that, even as we were coining our slogan, corporate publishing was quietly and surely disintegrating under the pressure of new technology. We did embrace the Internet early (1996!), but it wasn't until much later that I'd realized the majestic truth of the avantgardist impulse: we were ahead of the game because we didn't have any money! We had always accused the for-profit industry of pandering, and now we were right. If in the Age of Distribution just past, the game had been to get copies into the hands of the unwary and the presumed-innocent, in the Post-Distribution Age (now) the only requirement was veracity, artistic or not. Even integrity had returned, from whatever dark ethics dungeon it'd been confined to: one could maintain perfect integrity by communicating for free. Well, nearly. Everybody else communicated for mercenary reasons. Nonstop. Veracity and integrity were our *raisons d'être*. Of course, since time is the most valuable commodity, we were hardly doing anything "for free." We were just doing public service, like movie stars in rehab. And by we, I mean mostly me and Laura. Then just me and some poor assistant who got paid a measly allowance by the institution to "learn" the publishing ropes. What I'd been doing was penance for "teaching." They paid me to teach and I assuaged my guilty conscience by publishing literary assaults on institutions. I was the typical fin-de-siècle salaried beatnik. I regarded the smudged "ball" of my Selectric, now a display object, with the postcard of Allen Ginsberg, William Burroughs, and Philip Whalen, naked in a Colorado sauna, circa 1976. There it was: the museum of protest.

I made my way through the tottering towers of the print age. The surrealist collages on the wall and the collection of animal skulls hanging between them were covered with dust. The horse skull was also a clock: brass letters spelling out EXQUISITE CORPSE made up the hours. The hands pointed perpetually to X and I. Present from a smitten student. A huge nude painted lustily by a poet in the Eighties covered the basement window that didn't open. When did the window-that-doesn't-open become a feature of new buildings? Was it when the proletariat reached that Marxian alienation peak when suicide became the only alternative? A brass heart with my initials intertwined with those of a forgotten fan held down a stack of poetry from last semester.

I shoved aside an old telephone (landline, still working, no longer used, still blinking, scratched tape of "message machine" unlistened to) and found what I was looking for. The boom box. It stood atop of the very CD I was also looking for, No. 1 of 3 from the audio anthology "Poetry Speaks." On it was the recording of Ezra Pound I wanted Hillary Adams to hear. I would come clean to my soldier.

When I returned to the classroom, it looked like no one had moved. A couple of seats were empty, the last smokers, I suppose. Sure enough, Sylvia Minneaux, "Sylvie," and John Ferris, "Jack," returned from outside, smelling like humid petroleum air and smoke. There are times when the refineries work overtime here on the Gulf Coast, making the air practically flammable. Every time someone lights a cigarette I think, Boom! No text alert on that, eh?

I fiddled with the boom box. "You know what this is, don't you? Not an iPod. Haha." Did I laugh alone? Probably. I couldn't get the right cut. I kept pushing the Play button at random; various poets' voices came through, but no Pound. This CD contained many poets, including the first recording of poetry ever made, Sir Alfred Tennyson reading "The Charge of the Light Brigade" on Thomas Edison's wax cylinder device at the end of the nineteenth century. My old friend Stratis Haviaras, poetry librarian at Harvard, had first played this for me two decades before, along with an early recording of the Russian poet Vladimir Mayakovsky, the bard of the revolution who used to wow Moscow crowds with his voice. Oddly enough, Tennyson and Mayakovsky sounded alike, rumbly and boomy, as the needle jumped off the wax every time they came to the end of a line. Two poets more unalike one might not imagine. Together now in the wax. Happily, by the time Mr. Pound was committed to tape, things had improved. He sounded fierce and cranky, with just enough static in his voice to make you dread Time.

"I'm sorry, but does anyone in here know how these things work?"

Chloe Chamoix raised a weary hand, and sighed the sigh of youth faced with doddering old fucks.

"Chloe, please, would you be a dear and try to find cut number five for me? I'm a techno-idiot." Sure enough. It's called a *track*.

Chloe ambled over in tired jeans, not too fast, not too slow, not sure if bending over the boom box would show her ass to advantage, not sure even if she wanted to be in this class, even though it was a requirement if she wanted to graduate. She looked unsure of everything, but most of all she looked as if she couldn't remember what she was wearing. She'd just thrown something on in the morning, for chrissakes, nobody warned her that she had to *perform*. I'd seen the look. I wasn't impressed.

"There!" She hit Pound right on the nose. "Hugh Selwyn Mawberley": "*There died a myriad, / And of the best, among them, / For an old bitch gone in the teeth, / For a botched civilization, / Charm, smiling at the good mouth, / Quick eyes gone under earth's lid, / For two gross of broken statues, / For a few thousand battered books.*" The fierce Poundero thundered from beyond the grave in the voice that's caused nightmares for a century.

"The thing is, Hillary, this is Ezra Pound who was nearly hung for treason by the U.S. military after World War Two. He was a fascist and broadcast anti-American propaganda from Italy during the war. He was the Tokyo Rose . . ."

I looked at Hillary, who looked perfunctorily attentive but in truth, vacant. My God, she doesn't know who Tokyo Rose is. Does she even know about World War Two? Or One? The First World War, the "war to end all wars" that Pound was ranting against in his poem? Maybe all she knows is this war in Iraq, or as they are fond of calling it, "the war on terror." The endless war on terror, the ubiquitous Terror it created even as it fought it. That Hillary Adams might be killed for such figment, for such terror, was worse, a thousand times worse than dying for an old bitch gone in the teeth, for an old civilization . . . At least Pound believed that the old civilization might end and that a new one would rise . . . but this, this shadow of a shadow, this war without end . . .

"Hillary, did you hear that poem?"

"Something about an old bitch."

Laughter.

The laugh's on you, jokers.

"Well, yeah, but the old bitch was not a person, it was European civilization that Pound and his *young* friends believed must be destroyed. The civilization of parliaments, bankers, boring elections, representative democracy, the polite bourgeois and doomed proletarians that he felt didn't represent him or his generation. The civilization of polite salons, empty chatter, labor without joy, art without transcendence. Do you see what I'm saying?"

Hillary looked confused in her camouflage, a little girl in a big uniform, a twig in the wind, snappable, dispensable.

"He was antiwar, I guess."

Had to give her credit. She didn't flinch before the enemy. It was OK by her if someone was against the war, even her war. If it bothered her, she wasn't going to show it. She had worn the ROTC uniform for months now, and had passed

24

through the gauntlet of minority opinion on campus. She already knew that boys with long hair and languid eyes who wore *capoeira* pants and handmade Guatemalan pouches, and girls smelling of marijuana and sandalwood, did not approve of the war. She was OK with that. The majority saw to business.

It had been a grey, partly rainy day, when Laura and I visited Pound's grave on San Michele Island. When we'd gotten on at Giudecca it was raining, and only an old woman with an unfurled black umbrella got off the vaporetto at the cemetery island. We took a look back at Venice, barely visible in the rain, as the vaporetto vanished on its way to Murano. The old woman had already disappeared when we started wandering through the old boneyard. There was no one to greet us and the map on the church wall was incomprehensible. We meandered toward what looked like the most overgrown side of the island, assuming, correctly it turned out, that foreigners, especially Protestants, were buried together and rarely visited. We took shelter briefly under a portico open to the Lagoon until the rain eased up a bit. We found Igor Stravinsky and Sergei Diaghilev on either side of this archway. Hanging soggy from Diaghilev's stone were dozens of time-faded ballet slippers, but one pair looked new and petite in rosy freshness. We imagined the young ballerina, blushing mightily, looking furtively around before quickly hanging her slippers from the dance impresario's grave. It was a tradition. Stravinsky didn't look so well attended; his stone was untouched and solitary. We strolled by the graves of English ladies with many names dead at venerable ages, buried next to their female companions with whom they had lived in exile. And then, there they were, Ezra Pound and Olga Rudge, his mistress, under two square stones nearly smothered by a huge laurel bush. Soggy bits of paper hung from the wet bush, like prayers stuck into the cracks of the Wailing Wall. Unreadable now, these were poems left by visitors, readers of the poet, maybe even a new generation of the young convinced that the "old bitch gone in the teeth" needed more kicking.

We crouched on the ground and passed a notebook back and forth, writing old Ez a poem in a hurry, afraid that the rain might start up again. We filled a memorial page with panegyric and nostalgia, forgotten now, though I remember Laura writing at least two lines to Olga that ignored old Ez entirely. When I stuck our rolled-up *hommage* under the driest part of the bush, I noticed a not-so-soggy roll there, the work of another recent visitor. I unrolled it and read: "*Nothing matters but the quality of affection in the end.*" That was from one of Pound's later *Cantos*, after the war, when he entered into the deep silence that few outsiders breached before his death. There it was, the strange diction that prevented one from feeling wholehearted affection, despite the message. My generous memory quoted that line later as "*What matters in the end is the quality of affection,*" a gift to a man whose even most conciliatory and "human" line begins with "nothing" and ends with "the end."

"The truth, Hillary. How does he make you *feel?*"

"The truth? *Scared.* Is this, like, all poetry?"

"You mean is all poetry like this? No, I don't think so. He was an old cranky bastard, Pound was. We poets like him because he makes poetry scary and because he makes us feel that *writing poetry matters.* Do you have a favorite poet?"

"Well," she hesitated, then strode forward into the breach, "Shel Silverstein."

Many heads nodded in class. There were smiles. Life was hopeless. I eased off the gas. "Well, yes, pleasant and jingly and reassuring. Catchy. Have you outgrown him?"

That was mean. I try not to be mean in poetry class. Not out loud, anyway. It's my only rule. But she didn't notice. She nodded tentatively. "I think so. Maybe if there are some other poets between that and the scary guy . . . right?"

"There are thousands. In fact, there are thousands, not including myself, running interference between Shel and Ezra. But it's not boxing, you know. Some poets, even Pound, liked to box, but the main action goes on in the poems, in words. It takes courage to be a poet."

That was lame. I don't doubt that Pound had courage, but courage these days is watching the war on Fox News alone in a motel room. The sickness pulls at the bottom of your stomach and you're thinking of killing yourself. But you have class today! Move on. Three hours is not forever. Don't get killed, Hillary! But if it looks like you might, is it better to die reciting Shel Silverstein, the rosary, the Twenty-third Psalm, or screaming at the "old bitch" who sent you to war? The jury isn't out on that one. What am I doing here?

"Mr. Bennigan."

Bachmann, Balestrini, Baraka, Beckett, Bei Dao, Bernstein, Berrigan, Blackburn, Brecht, Breton, Burroughs, and more Bs than that. An embarrassment of riches. I'd known half those people and it'd take me years to tell half of what I know. The other half I'd read up on and heard stories about, and just remembering titles or the people who'd known them would take more years than I have. I am not trying to get out of the teaching racket to write my memoirs. Still, a bunch of my co-generationists are publishing theirs and getting everything wrong. And that's while trying to get everything right without forgetting the memoirist's first duty, which is to place him/herself at the center of historical things. I'd already written two memoirs in my youth, precisely in order to prevent these later memoirs from claiming everything. In other words, I'd already invented the past these co-generationists were so painstakingly (and wrongly!) reassembling. Only my dead friends were not writing memoirs these days, which was a boon to scholars. Biographies are the mushrooms du jour.

There was a hint of sweet revenge in handing over a dead poet to someone like Bennigan, who knew nothing about poetry, but loved to make people laugh. In an act of uncalled-for perversity I could hand the funny guy a grim Ghost-Companion (G-C from now on) that would knock the fun out of him, but why? Class clowns don't bother me. I used to be one. What, for instance, would poor Bennigan do if I paired him with Amiri Baraka, whose prevailing view of life is murderous rage, relieved only now and then by some deeply bitter inside joke? A sweet, funny man, actually, I keep running into him at airports, just after seeing one of his old wives or girlfriends, coincidentally. He greets me, I greet him, I think: Jeezus, this guy is a communist! He was also a black nationalist who scared the shit out of me in 1968 when he had his New Jersey acting troupe fire guns into the darkness of a theater where I'd gone with a bunch of his old white friends to see what he was up to after years of not speaking to white people. Happily, the lights came back on and the whole thing did turn out to be a *play*, after all, not the mass murder of the avantgarde as I had feared. Now he was a professor, like all of us. Just retired. Would Bennigan G-C'd by Baraka become a communist, a black nationalist, a horny avantgardist, a prophet from New Jersey? I doubt it, but neither would he understand what was happening to him as he made his way through the jagged shards of the man's poesy. He would sulk and trade for another G-C and land right in the arms of Charles Bernstein, a master ironist. Oy! What to do with Bennigan? I didn't want to offer him

Ted Berrigan, because Ted is my own G-C. Nor would he have much use for André Breton, who'd smother his collegiate wit under a fiery blanket of surrealism. Brecht might make a proletarian out of him yet. Yes, that was it. Bertolt Brecht. Short poems, lotsa common sense. Paul Blackburn wouldn't be bad either: funny man, Sagittarian, translator of troubadours, killed by chain-smoked Gauloises, a sweetheart.

"Awright, Bennigan, Brecht heads, Blackburn tails."

He called tails. I flipped the quarter, came up tails. I was actually relieved. I'd been afraid it would come up Brecht and then I'd have to revisit all that history. East Germany. Ugh. I'd just read Joel Agee's memoir of growing up in East Germany, but that wasn't as bad as some of the other books I'd read about the place. And to think that when I was growing up in Romania we thought East Germany was paradise! They had sausages and oranges there and they could escape to the West!

"Paul Blackburn was an intense, funny man who lived downtown in New York on East 7th Street, right next door to McSorley's Old Ale House, which was the first all-male business the radical feminists took on in the late Sixties. They just stormed right in and ordered beer. Paul was in Provence and in Spain a lot, and a guy named George Kendall leased his apartment from him and had a poker night for the guys. I used to play poker there with Ted Berrigan and Dick Gallup and some other guys."

I had just been a kid, their age really, and never having any money, I lost my three poker dollars pretty fast, and then went to the kitchen, where I made out with Kendall's wife Lucy, who was bored. I mean, right downstairs raging feminists were breaking down the gender barrier, and up here she was just making drinks for the guys. No wonder she let me feel her up and kiss her, even though I was just a kid. Later she ran off with an antiwar activist who packed heat, but George came after *me* with a baseball bat. Wrong guy, I screamed, just in time for the bat to swing away from my head. It makes one wonder if the past is nothing but a bunch of lucky misses from angry guys' bats.

"Paul Blackburn is a great poet and he put the troubadour lyrics into very cool English, and wrote his own imitations of troubadour poems, things like *sirventes* and *aubades*. *Sirventes* are curses that the troubadours flung at the castle when they were thrown out of noble ladies' beds because their crusader-knight husbands were coming back. The ladies usually had advance notice that a gaggle of crusader-knights had been spotted returning home after a dozen years or so of pillaging around Jerusalem, so they rounded up the poets in a hurry and saw them out of the castles, even as the locksmiths worked fast to weld back their chastity belts. The poets flung *sirventes* at the receding castle. When things were good, flames roaring in the stone fireplace, an oak barrel of wine just tapped, the ladies all pink and coy, the poets wrote *aubades*, which are a form of verse written at dawn after a night of lovemaking. Paul Blackburn translated both curses, *sirventes*, and white-night odes, *aubades*, and he wrote his own, too. One of them he wrote after living through a cold clammy winter in Toulouse: '*I have made a sirventes / against the city of Toulouse / and it cost me plenty of garlic!*' I may be paraphrasing, Bennigan, but I think that it's in the same poem that he speaks with a cold and calls his nose 'doze,' which is how you say 'nose' when you have a cold. Brilliant. So he's all yours to research, man. Go to the library, look him up online, call people who knew him. He died in the Seventies, but you make an ally of his ghost, it will be like having your own knight-at-arms by your side!"

Bennigan was entranced. Everybody else seemed to me to be texting under their desks, against express orders. I brought *Poems for the Millennium, Volume Two* sharply down on the desk. If any texting was going to go on here, it would be out of the textbook! They started. Their thumbs froze. No, they weren't texting. There was no text-message alert. They just kept their hands down there to defend their genitals, under attack from poets.

"Matthew Borden! Ah, Matt Borden! Heir to a fortune! Like William Burroughs or James Merrill?" He didn't look like he knew what I was talking about, but I wasn't taking any chances with Matt Borden. He'd gotten me once. A flame might shoot out of that ball of hair anytime.

"William Burroughs," he said

"You mean, rich like Burroughs, or do you want him for a Ghost-Companion?"

"Companion."

"For his cool factor? Bands named after his books?"

"Neither. He looks like my dad, even speaks like that. When my dad's had a scotch, he's off on riffs most reminiscent of Mr. Burroughs from St. Louis. I heard him read from *Naked Lunch*, I have the vinyl record. But I didn't know he wrote poetry."

Matt Borden was cool and slick. Vinyl. Burroughs. What's next? John Giorno? Dial-A-Poem? How deep into the past did this milk fortune heir go? Borden was not the first student in "Introduction to Writing Poetry" to startle me with unexpected knowledge of the obscure worlds of literature, but he was the first to have a grandmother who'd been friends with Queen Marie and was buried inside a statue.

"Burroughs did write what we might call poetry, even if it didn't look conventional. Maybe that's all he wrote. And letters. Sure, he made up characters like Dr. Benway, and used historical persons for philosophical reasons, but his prose is poetry-thick and funny. I wonder what it'd be like to have him rumble in your ear when you don't have a thought in your head. He'd make one hell of a G-C! And then there is the drug factor . . ."

"I'm kinda curious about that." Borden's face came out from under his hair, dreamy gaze aimed in my general direction. "I never did anything, except for a toke or two at a party, but I appreciate expert opinion."

The class snickered. Experience. Half, if not all, felt superior. They'd toked longer, they'd had glue, mushrooms, cocaine, Adderall, Vicodin, and salvia. But they didn't have a family cemetery in a decommisioned nuclear silo.

"I'm not sure it's necessary to experience the drug thing to enjoy Burroughs. He was an expert, you're right about that. Maybe he did drugs so his readers wouldn't have to." I don't push drugs. They'd been mainstream for years and useless to the current mind as far as I could tell. I have to qualify this because I don't know what the current mind might be hatching, but judging by Facebook, not much. All drugs seemed to be party drugs now, leading to where party drugs always lead: to hangovers. If anybody retrieved a grand insight from an out-of-body-on-drugs experience now, I'd seen no expression of it. Of course, come to think of it, I never saw much expression of my generation's grand insights, either, though I've read, watched, and heard plenty of complaints about the impossibility of expressing such insights. Maybe it was the impossibility of expressing such insights that led to such a flowering of silly poetry and art in the last three decades! Impossibility, your name is Poetry! But I have even less sympathy for the hangovers of today's young. I'd had my share of hangovers, and the charm was gone when the amount of spiritual benefit exceeded by far the time needed to recover.

When a beatific vision lasts three minutes and the hangover three days, a serious man must draw a budget. Even sex, the earthly payoff, has not left behind enough postcoital memory to sustain an ongoing libidinal store. I was profligate to say the least, but I don't blame drugs. My father's genes had doubtlessly more to do with my appetite than Ecstasy or cocaine. An exposed thigh for my benefit in a dingy classroom does me better and longer now than a stoned/drunken fuck in a bar bathroom during a poetry reading by the enemy in 1976. That was the year of the bicentennial when my enemies started reading in bars with unisex toilets, just before AIDS showed up. Two hundred years of liberty and look where we fucked! Poetry readings in those days featured two poets, and there was a ten-minute break between poets. The trick was to leave unobtrusively with a lively like-minded person ten minutes *before* the break, lay a few lines of coke on top of the toilet, have sex, and be done by the break so there wouldn't be a line shuffling outside, bladders full of annoyed piss. Annoyed by the poetry. Sometimes people without drugs would wander out of the audience to pee or pretend to pee, whatever, just to get away from the grating voice on stage. Sometimes we'd hear a knock, and knowing full well that it wasn't the break yet, I'd lean back and unlatch the rickety lock (when there was one) and a startled third party would find herself there, unsure about what to do at the sight of lines of coke on top of the stall and a girl with her legs around a man's hips, his pants down to his ankles. The intruder would usually walk away, unless it was another poet of the drugs-and-sex persuasion, and she/he would laugh, so we'd let her/him in, and then I'd lock the door again. The her/him business was quite solemn at that time, and I'm only bringing it up to illustrate the vertiginous descent of language from the psychedelic explorations of the late Sixties when everything was an "it" to the violent aggressivity of a later decade when "me" (whether him or her) showed up. Why bring up these things, indeed, but try to understand, poetry class, that drugs were how the times themselves understood their temporality. Drugs were how the zeitgeist got to know itself, to become conscious of its shapes and forms. Burroughs was a heroin junkie in the 1950s, an age as remote to me as the 1970s is to my students. He was addicted to the lows of the dreamworld, where he could be stock-still like a black and white photograph. In the background you could still see Vienna, Dr. Freud, Europe, Nazis. Mr. Burroughs watched it all with the blank opiate stare of his six pairs of eyes (one pair at the back of his head) and wrote with increasing voraciousness as the Fifties receded and his acolytes showed up, with benzedrine to make a goofball from. Heroin is making a comeback, so maybe a new kind of fanciful Fifties mood is too, but I'm quite sure that your dreams will be neither funny nor spectacular because you are not William Burroughs. You are high and empty like Byzantine icons. And you're going to OD.

I have a lot of dead friends.

"Matt," I said, "you don't suppose that there might be a spare silo in the vicinity of your family boneyard? It just occurred to me that many poets die indigent, and that if they had a poet's silo they could be buried in there with all their books on shelves around them. Young poets would come to visit and the place'd become a tourist attraction. Some of them might drop by to see your grandmother Diana, and that might lead them to the Queen Marie museum in Washington. Wouldn't *that* be a project? Your grandma and the Queen of Romania would be such exotic magnets for poetry tourists! Not to speak of the convenience of having all the poets not already buried in Paris interred in one place for convenient teaching. A university is sure to spring up around this poets' Arlington, our own American-contemporary Westminster Abbey. You must ask your G-C for advice in this matter. William Burroughs was a practical man, he'd inherited it from his grandfather, the inventor of the Burroughs adding machine."

D.B. "Mr. Dynamite," a Louisiana painter, went to the viewing of the body in Lawrence, Kansas, when the writer died in 1997. Unobserved, he slipped an automatic pistol in the pants pocket of the impeccable suit Burroughs wore in the casket. The casket was then closed and the funeral cortege drove off to St. Louis for the burial, four hours away. Some of the mourners were high and they got hungry halfway through the trip, so it was decided, cell phone to hearse, to stop at a McDonald's. As the cars with the hearse at the head pulled into the McDonald's parking lot, a group of Goth high schoolers were lounging about the place, smoking cigarettes. A sixteen-year-old boy was sitting cross-legged on the sidewalk reading a book. Mr. Dynamite, the painter, looked to see what the book was. It was *The Beat Reader*, an anthology of writings by the Beats. "What are you reading?" asked D.B. "This guy, William Burroughs," the kid said disdainfully, sure that the old geezer in the cheap suit before him would have no idea what planet was being discussed. Taking his time, Mr. Dynamite lit a cigarette, looked at the top of the boy's head, and waited until the boy looked up. When the boy did, the painter pointed to the hearse: "We've got him in there. Wanna come to the funeral? Your friends can, too." Sure enough. The kids crowded into the various cars and the party got merrier as they drove on to the Bellefontaine Cemetery, where there was a spirited ceremony as the body took its place in the family crypt where reposed also William Seward Burroughs, William's grandfather.

It rained as the cortege made its way back to Lawrence. The kids were dropped off back at the McDonald's parking lot. The writer's body remained under the ground and was quiet, as Burroughs himself had often been. But now comes the strange part: inside the body there was a riot as nature went to work. Gases began rising in decomposition, like riffs to be typed later on the typewriter Burroughs never renounced, even long after computers became writerly tools. Two months later, let's say, the ferment reached the fully loaded pistol in the pocket and squeezed out a round. The bullet ricocheted off the vault wall and sped through the tomb's opening to meet a lone visitor, looking for the grave of the writer with Google Earth on the iPhone in his hand. As he pored over Google Earth he stood directly across from the crypt, where the bullet found him. Cold case. Never solved. Don't even try. I made it up. But Burroughs did shoot his wife, née Joan Vollmer, in the head during a game of William Tell and Apple. Reputed to be a crack shot, he'd played the game before, but this time, he missed. Years later, he would do a commercial for Apple computers, and I wonder what he thought of the irony. The shooting of the tourist was just as accidental, but this time he wasn't drunk as he'd been when he mistakenly shot his beloved Joan. This time he was dead, just a corpse with a gun. Make what you will of it, but during the last decades of his life, Burroughs shot at targets that were later displayed in museums. Art knows everything. Your other assignment, I could tell the class, is to answer in sonnet-form the questions "Can the dead kill?" and "What is Art?" I assigned that one to myself. Some assignments are just too hard.

"That would be a *great* project," Matt said, able to contain his enthusiasm, "we own about ten decomissioned nuclear silos!" Without even trying, I'd coaxed the businessman out of him. Don't tell me it's not genetic. "I'll talk to my dad."

I was silent for an uncomfortably long time. The class shifted, pens straightened, eyes glazed, fingers tapped on knees under desks, etc. Am I being depressing? Being young is bad enough. But if I let them write whatever they want, instead of insisting on the mortal gravity of the art they'd signed up for, everything they'd write would be about suicide and mass murder. There is nothing wrong with being depressing from *experience*. I was preventing them from being macabre from *pretense*. They are young, these people, but not above extorting emotions from fake traumas.

"Well, go ahead, Matt, use your cell phone. I'm making an exception to the no-cell rule. Call your dad."

"What? Call my dad now? I doubt it. It's delicate."

I can imagine. Hordes of riffraff running around nuclear silos in the Badlands with iPhones trying to find dead poets. The peace of the Dakotas shattered. Dad furious. Sells farm to Ted Turner, moves operations to Alaska where the fishing is better. Better approach Ted Turner ahead of time on this one. There might already be old nuke silos on the vast neighboring acres where his buffalos roam. *Diana the Huntress?* The image struck me again. I saw her standing at the bottom of the nuclear silo where a lone soldier once stood before a console and a telephone, reading endless novels, waiting for his one moment of work when the phone would ring. He'd pick up the phone and push the button that would annihilate Moscow. What is it that Diana the Huntress is aiming the bronze arrow in her taut bow at? Not Moscow, surely. Maybe her arrow is aimed at her own family, that philistine bunch of milk farmers who know nothing of poetry. Or maybe she's aiming it at the military-industrial complex whose vacated nuclear heart she is now inhabiting. Or maybe she is aiming it at the ghostly presence of the solitary soldier who read Dostoyevsky to pass the time. What a job that young man had! There are no other jobs exactly like that, but in a room at the headquarters of Christian Science in Boston someone waits for a white phone to ring: it's a dedicated line leading to only one other phone, also white, resting inside the crypt of the Christian Science founder Mary Baker Eddy. On her deathbed she told her followers that when the time came for her resurrection, she'd call from the grave. The living receptionist waits. It's the best job she's ever had. She reads Jane Austen. I wondered where inside the sculpture of Diana was the Borden heiress. Was she molded to the inside of the cast, or was there just an urn resting on an interior platform at pelvis level, at the widest part? At some point in the semester, when I know Matt better, I'll ask. It's a fair guess, however, that inside everything hollow hides something, especially inside sculptures. Only sculptors abhor a vacuum more than nature. No empty pockets.

"Fine, Matt. You adopt William Burroughs and let him guide and advise you. Report on conversation with dad, you can e-mail me before class as to what he said, and I'll be glad to talk to him myself if he's interested. But enough of this funerary business, class. Poets are one thing, they are human, but does anyone happen to know where old *computers* are buried? Does *anyone* know? Jillions of toxic machines are retired every few minutes! Where in the world do they go? The nuclear waste question is still being fought over. The people in Nevada don't want nuclear waste. Neither does anyone else. Meanwhile, the radioactive material lies in lead caskets in some of our most beautiful places, Prairie Island for instance, indigenous Lakota land between Wisconsin and Minnesota in the Mississippi River, causing cancer in every member of the tribe. The eagles are coming back, but cancer spreads there . . . even the eagles get it. And if that's bad, the hard plastic and toxins of your PC are just as bad, but nobody knows where they chuck it . . . or old cell phones . . . where do they put those?"

"In live volcanoes?" That was from Chloe Chamoix, the next person, as it happens, in line for receiving a G-C.

I don't want answers to questions posed by my ranting. But sometimes they seem *sensible*. Live volcanoes! This was *sensible*. I remember looking down into snaking rivers of red lava below the village of Volcano on the Big Island in Hawaii. I'd read my poetry to a small audience that included a blind old man with long white hair and a 300-pound Maori lesbian from New Zealand, and now we were all naked, squeezed in a muddy crack on the volcano lip, drinking gin and smoking Rasta-sized spliffs of Mowie-Zowie, and looking down into the flames. When Dr. Dunsford, the New Zealand lesbian scholar, finished the gin, she tossed the bottle into the furnace below and chanted something in the Maori language that, roughly translated, was: "Take this gin, Pele!" It was the only thing that the Goddess of Volcanoes and Fire would accept, she explained: gin bottles. Anything else and your ass is barbecue. No old computers, for sure. There was a sky full of stars overhead and the scent of ginger flowers saturated the brisk air. Die now, I ordered myself. The slightest tremor of the earthquakes that regularly rocked the small village of Volcano would have sent us hurtling into Pele's fiery arms. No such luck. Returned to the homeland. Am teaching Intro to Poetry Writing.

Chloe now brought up something I'd forgotten. "The man who visited graves of poets and was killed . . . his detective took poetry class, right? I know you said that she didn't solve the case, but what was the name of her teacher again, Sharon . . . ?"

"Sharon Mesmer," I filled in. I'd forgotten all about that man, because I'd made him up. That visitor to poets' graves had been me, but I sometimes feel that it's unfair to have so much experience, so I distribute it among characters. "Yes, Sharon Mesmer, who, just like William Burroughs and Mr. Borden here, is the grandchild of a famous person, Dr. Mesmer, from whom we derive the word *mesmerism*. One of the *tools of poetry*—" I pointed to the blackboard, "is *susceptibility to hypnotism. Mesmerism* means *fascination*, but it can also mean *hypnotism*. Dr. Mesmer believed that by passing magnets over a sick person he would realign their inner fluids and heal them. He later found that by just passing his hands over a sick person he could obtain the same result. How *fascinating* is that?"

"Yes, but I was wondering if the detective wrote *good poetry* after she took the class . . . did she learn to be a poet? Can you be a good poet and a lousy detective?"

Good question. "I'm not sure, but we can find out. Detective Flores went on to become captain of her precinct, but was fired under Giuliani. About her poetry I don't know." I reached for my cell phone, which I'd shut down along with everyone else at the start of the class. "We can ask Professor Mesmer, her teacher, whose personal number I have in my cell. Should we?"

"Sure!" Chloe was amused.

Class wakes up. Yeah. Call.

I'm at a crossroads here. Do I call a real person to ask about an imaginary character she has never met? I do know Sharon Mesmer, and she *is* mesmerizing. I first met her long ago in Chicago, where I'd gone to give a poetry reading. I had planned to meet Sharon, who was only seventeen years old then, in a coffee shop, but I came down with the flu. I shook and threw up and was shivering with fever in my hotel room, so I called to cancel. But instead of canceling, I told her that she should come to my hotel room because I was sick. I had something of a reputation in those days, and Sharon was rumored to be a considerable beauty, so the whole thing must have sounded fishy because when she showed up, and she did, she came with a retinue of grim Chicago poets wearing leather jackets doing their best to impersonate thugs. I sniffled through a painful interview, amused by my own legend, but in the end I'm not sure that it was a good idea to bring thugs. I might have been healed if she'd come alone. Her grandfather might have burst through her to lay hands on me.

Yes. I looked at my cell phone. I didn't turn it on and missed, again, the text-message alert test that might prevent something like the tragedy at Virginia Tech, where that insane creative writing student massacred 32 people on April 16, 2007.

"On the other hand, we don't have so much time now. I should assign you the rest of your G-Cs, and then you can hurry to acquire your poetry tools and start applying the rules for your assignments."

I could touch their disappointment: no phone call to give them a break, and no break, as far as they could tell. They needed to pee. I knew that they needed to pee. They knew that they needed to pee. Their bladders were ready to burst. Ah, merciless poetry! I saw myself covered in the golden showers of their bursting bladders. No, I'm not a pervert. Ask anybody.

"Chloe . . . Cage, Celan, Cardenal, Cruz, Césaire, Coolidge, Corso, Creeley, Cortez . . . oh, boy! The world before

you, diamonds, sapphires, lightning bolts, barbells ... Do
you recognize any of the names?' She nodded no. "What do
you like, Chloe? I mean, what is your most favorite thing in
the world?"

I'd become concerned suddenly that Chloe, with her
straight black hair and the small diamond in her left nostril
and cat-eye glasses, was too fragile to take on the weight of
any of those male poets (or even of the sole woman, Jayne
Cortez), though clearly she enjoyed a modicum of pain. Her
pretty face was sleepy, fundamentally, not from a night's lack
of it, but from birth. Face slightly elongated like a milk tear.
I could see rows of hearts magic-markered in colors in the
notebook open before her. What dream was I about to wake
her up from?

"My hammock, I love my hammock. We live on False
River in the country and I go home any time I can, just to lie
in the hammock ..."

Sweet Jesus breezes. I could see her, in late afternoon, fast
asleep in her hammock, textbook fallen in the grass below
her, one of her hands dangling down ... watched from the
river bank by an alligator in love. Her faithful pointer was
asleep too, though his ear twitched now and then to let the
alligator, who had no evil intentions, know that he was
aware of his presence. The alligator's puppy love didn't
worry the pointer. The bucolic world had an understanding
when it came to Chloe: it spoiled her.

"Let's say now that some emergency, maybe even a historical one, happens. This terrible thing, maybe a hurricane
that swallows the coast, or an atomic explosion, or violent
anti-French sentiment ... Chamoix is French, right?"

"Cajun, actually."

"OK, so something like that, an anti-Cajun sentiment ...
your people were expelled once from Canada, that's how

42

they came to be here in Louisiana, right? It happened once, it can happen again. Let's say that a thing like that happens, and you have to leave home and live in another country, learn to speak a different language, marry a foreign man, have children who don't speak your language anymore . . . suppose that you'll never see your beloved hammock again . . ."

Chloe's eyes started clouding: any moment now, a tear as sweet as her whole person might fall. I'd drink it. I swear, I'd get up and drink it. I wanted to stop that tear, but I couldn't. I was the teacher, the poetry teacher, and I had a job to do. The tear didn't fall.

"OK, Chloe, we are just imagining, but I can see that you are *empathic*, which means that you can feel what others feel, so I decided to assign to you the great Martinican poet Aimé Césaire. Away from his birthplace, Césaire had a terrible longing for his home on the beautiful island of Martinique. He didn't know if he'd ever be able to return. It was chilly and cold in Paris, so when one of his fellow students invited him to spend the winter break with his family on the island of Martinka in Yugoslavia, Césaire was happy. On Martinka, the name of which reminded him of Martinique, he wrote about his longing for home in a beautiful long poem entitled *Cahier d'un retour au pays natal—A Notebook of a Return to My Native Country*, but I'm sure you know the French. This long poem is all about the terrible feeling that he would never lie in his beloved hammock again, and that he had to use his *memory* to return there."

"That sounds doable," said Chloe, definitively pulling back her potential tear, for which resolve I was grateful, because it's unbecoming for a teacher to rise from his seat to drink a pupil's tear, no matter how strong the urge.

I didn't tell Chloe that Aimé Césaire returned to Martinique where, together with the poets Léopold Senghor of Senegal and Léon Damas, he conceived the Négritude movement, a poetic and political force that was at the source of later African and Black Power movements. His friend Léopold Senghor became president of the Republic of Senegal, and Césaire himself, supported by the French Communist party, became the leader of the left-wing party that ruled Martinique for most of the twentieth century. Césaire was a four-term mayor of Martinique's capital city, Fort-de-France, where I met him in 2001.

Fort-de-France is a pretty serious hellhole, a cross between Detroit and New Orleans, without the industrial (past) glory of Detroit or the *joie de vivre* of New Orleans. Across from the mayoral palace, a decaying old colonial building, where Laura and I were going to meet the poet in the office he still kept there, was a noisy, heavily trafficked boulevard. Dividing this diesel-choked road was a sorry median strip, a kind of ratty park with a few benches and neglected statues of French colonial heroes and, of newer vintage, African giants of liberty who looked even more forlorn. Most prominent among these stone notables was a giant statue of Josephine Bonaparte, whose head was missing. A dribbly line of red paint ran down from her neck to her proud stone bosom. Our rental car died right in her proximity, so we were stopped hopelessly in the traffic, looking up at the headless giant, without a clue as to what to do next. Happily, as is often the case in poor countries, a crowd of experts gathered about the car and helped us push it onto the median, right under the pedestal of Napoleon's wife. I opened the hood and several would-be mechanics began to venture opinions in Martinican French and Creole. After a noisy argument having to do with spark plugs, as well as the mysteries of Citroen, an older gent with a well-trimmed mustache shoved the experts aside, reached into the engine, did something, and the car started. A miracle, a blessing. I took out my wallet to reward the good Samaritan, but he waved my money away. "It's hard to find entertainment in Fort-de-France these days ... the tourists don't come. It's a horrible, dangerous city." Seeing me look up at Josephine, he explained: "Her head is being held hostage by radicals. When Martinique gains independence from France, they promise to return the head." When Laura laughed, he said, "You are the first American tourists in Martinique in many years!" I told him that we had come to interview the country's famous poet, Aimé Césaire. My poetic pride got no approval from him. In fact, he spit, and made the face one makes when the devil is mentioned. "*Merde, merde,*" he said, "he is why this city is *merde,* this country is *merde,* and all that it could be is *merde.*" "But the poetry ..." I insisted. "The poetry ... everyone in this country writes poetry! Maybe if they could fix an engine and not write so much poetry, things might be less *merde.*" We took our leave of the elderly lawyer, who, before resuming his stroll, handed me his card. "Not in practice any longer. *Merde* laws in this *merde* city."

Marie Josèphe Rose Tascher de la Pagerie, born to French sugar planters in Martinique, was married to a young French noble in Paris who lost his head to the guillotine. Josephine was scheduled to follow him to the scaffold, but the Terror ended suddenly, and she found herself a young widow and mother, who wanted more than anything else to party. She became one of the wild ladies of Paris who had escaped execution, a stroke of luck they celebrated by wearing red ribbons around their necks, right at the place where their heads might have been severed. They celebrated by flaunting their charms at nightly balls that stretched into the morning, and it was at one of these balls that Josephine met army sergeant

Bonaparte, who fell in love and married her and who loved her so much that he relented to her demand to prolong the institution of slavery in Martinique twenty-five years after it had been abolished in Europe and its colonies. For love of Josephine, the emperor sacrificed one of his most cherished principles. No wonder her head was missing, guillotined post mortem by the still-angry descendants of slaves who didn't have to be slaves. Those twenty-five years explained a lot about Martinique. A green and vertiginous volcanic island, Martinique is the southernmost point of a bloody colonial route for trading slaves, rum, and sugar. The northernmost point of the route was New Orleans, America's most brutal slave market. If I were a Martinican radical I wouldn't return Josephine's head, either: I'd impale it on a long pole and parade it on Independence Day. As it is, the radicals are a small group, and Martinique still consists of sugarcane and banana plantations overseen by wealthy French planters from fabulous mansions with views of the sea. The planters' grandchildren spend enchanting vacations swimming in the calm bay of "Josephine's bathtub," playing tennis and flirting with the black gardeners and picnicking in private zoos among tamed exotic birds and animals. Below, in the sugarcane and banana fields, the laborers work with machetes, just like their ancestors, stopping under the hot sun only for a minute when one of them is bitten by a fer-de-lance, reputedly the world's most poisonous snake. After the body is taken away, they resume their work. In the evening they line up in front of the store in their village for a baguette, free thanks to French socialism. Tall, beautiful women with heads wrapped in bright African scarves and muscular, tired men walk in the fading light to their shacks, baguettes sticking out from under their arms like lances. The Martinique Tourism Bureau had started, at the time of our visit, the construction of fake fishing villages for tourists. Just behind these simulacra, mobbed by August vacationers from *la mère patrie*, the real villages simmer with rage.

Aimé Césaire was such a tall, beautiful man, even in his early nineties, that a sigh of admiration floated from Laura. I know my woman. She can appreciate a fine physique. Nor was the great poet unaware of hers. His middle-aged secretary, a broad-shouldered man a good six inches shorter than the poet, led us to his sunny office and warned us not "to take too much of his time, maybe fifteen minutes, he tires easily." If he did tire, it wasn't evident. Césaire crunched my hand in a powerful grip and took in Laura at a glance, like a lion. "What language would you prefer?" I asked him, "French or English?" He laughed, "French or Creole!" So French it was. For the better part of the next two hours he reminisced about his youth, about his encounters with surrealists, about André Breton, about Tristan Tzara, and, above all, about his love for eastern Europe and the island of Martinka, where he'd experienced the greatest longing for Martinique. He confessed that he no longer gave interviews, in fact had turned down the *New York Times* the week before, but my being from Romania had persuaded him to see me. Every time he showed signs of being tired, or when his secretary seated nearby gave him a reproachful look, he took a look at Laura, who made sure to cross her legs as often as possible. She wore a short skirt and exuded her usual intoxicating aroma of sex and intelligence. His eyes glittered, her eyes glittered. She took in every word avidly, but she speaks not an iota of French. What he said was that his leadership saved Martinique from ruin because he had kept the province within France, while obtaining the maximum autonomy for his people. I gave him a copy of my book, *The Hole in the Flag: A Romanian Exile's Story of Return and Revolu-*

47

tion, about my own return from exile to my birthplace, after the failure of communism. I was afraid that my evident lack of sympathy for the left might stand between us. He read my dedication to him and the book's jacket and smiled. Only Laura's legs stood between us, literally. A bridge (two bridges) between opposing ideologies. He was too old and too shrewd to argue something as sterile as ideology. Besides, he had renounced communism in 1956, after the Soviet invasion of Czechoslovakia, and had remained faithful only to Martinique and socialism. Given a chance, he'd renounce that, for the woman. In this, he was a poet through and through, my brother, *mon frère*. At long last, his secretary's worries caused him to stand. We led the poet out and parted after a long goodbye and a fiery embrace (of Laura).

"As far as I know, he's alive still," I told Chloe. "On page 75 of your textbook you'll find the lines '*I hook on like devil's guts / or uncoil piranha-like.*' Those are the feelings of a man banished from his hammock."

"I don't know, he feels a little heavy for me," said Chloe

"Possibly, but think of it this way. Your hammock on False River is tied between two oak trees that may have well been there when the land was a slave plantation."

"That's for sure, those trees are three hundred years old, and the ruins of the plantation are still there . . . it was burnt by Union soldiers in the Civil War. If I ever get rich, I'll rebuild it."

"There you are. History links Martinique to your ruins in a straight line! And if you do get rich, surely not through poetry, but by some other means not yet visible, I advise you to dedicate a room of your rebuilt plantation house to Aimé Césaire . . ."

"It's a deal!" Chloe chuckled. The class looked uneasy.

Not all of them were plantation-worshippers, and Anita Washington was black.

"Jason Jacob."

Jason Jacob, "JJ," looked both respectful and ironic. He sported a scraggly reddish beard and his eyes sparkled with something like compassion tinged by resolve. If I make him sound like Leon Trotsky, it is because he looked very much like young Trotsky. Jewish, swift, and, perhaps, resolute. I suspected too that his parents were hippies, or at least his mother was. In that case, the resolve I read there might be just a look.

First impressions are often wrong. This one wasn't. "JJ" was a young spawn of hippies with artistic inclinations. He had a social conscience. His resolve was yet to be determined.

He said: "I'll take any poet who can teach me how to end the war."

Oh, boy. I glanced at Hillary for a reaction. She looked cool under fire. *Too* cool. Should Hillary now call him unpatriotic and start a harangue, I'd have to do what I've done dozens of time over the years: referee. One year, albeit in an upper-level course subscribed to by poetry veterans at least three years older, I had a Christian anti-abortion activist, author of the poem "Six Dead Fetuses," go mano-a-mano against a feisty lesbian, author of "A Guide to Lesbian Sex," consisting of twelve numbered lines (positions) for the beginner lesbian, such as "Kiss mouth after briefly kissing cunt to get the taste of each other." I barely disentangled them before they got physical (luckily they sat at different ends of the class). It didn't help that a devil's advocate, a chunky blond boy raised on MTV, cried out in glee "Bitch Fight!" I hoped I wouldn't have to referee between my young warrior and tender Trotsky.

I didn't. Different times, other creatures. "JJ" turned to Hillary and said, "It's my opinion, that's all." She nodded. Understood. And something passed between them. Romance always flourishes in poetry classes. So many confessions, so much emotion, such pressurized ideas!

"JJ, I'm looking at Joyce, Jabès, Jandl, Jacob, and Jorn, but I can't resist your homonymity. I'm bonding you to Max Jacob, French poet, born Jewish, converted to Catholicism by Jacques Maritain, took up monastic life, invented the cubist poem, aka the prose poem, was arrested and deported by the Nazis and killed right before the end of the war. The Second World War," I hastened to add. "If you're against war now, just wait till you read Jacob."

"Well, there are wars and wars," JJ said. "The Second World War was justified."

I wasn't going to get into that. I love Max Jacob. I hoped young Trotsky would, too. I even translated some poems by Max Jacob from the French, and I always loved his worldly explanation of why he'd become a Catholic monk: "I love picking up my robe when I walk up stairs," he's said to have said, making him instantly chic. The real reason is in one of the poems I'd translated, where he has a vision of the Virgin in a beam of light in the window of his mansard. I'd always thought that should I become suddenly illuminated by other-worldly belief it would happen the way it happened to Max Jacob. A holy vision in a dingy place in a great city, Paris, on a clouded afternoon broken only by that ray of light. What I find impossible to conceive of is the suddenness. I can see that there are mysteries, I *have* seen them, but they were symmetrical and made sense, there was nothing in a hurry about the magical clockworks of the universe. Of course, a stroke could change all that. Maybe. I don't like the idea of strokes unless they kill you on the spot. A paralyzing stroke would be a mighty mean thing on the part of the marvelous clockworks, but I'm sure that there'd be nothing personal about it. Sometimes, time wacks out for no reason apparent to the whackee, like it did on my cell phone. *Memento mori* means not only "remember death," but also "glitch." That's sort of the way I translated Max Jacob, following the example of my G-C Ted Berrigan, who rendered "*c'est la vie*" as "that's the breaks." Still, a sudden conversion beats a sudden death. Should *that* happen I would no longer find instant revelation impossible, though my melancholy would know no bounds.

The sound of my own sadness kicked my ass. Hurry up.

"Beatrice Garland!"

How's that for a poetic name? Overly poetic name. Ultra. She was the mop-headed redhead in ripped jeans. At some point she'd taken off a jeans jacket and flung it at her feet. On the bare shoulder of her plump white arm was tattooed a black cat with green eyes. Wearing what I think is called a "wife-beater," she looked the picture of a chic young punk. I could see her slouched on a late-night sofa drinking beer with a foot in her girlfriend's crotch. A loud chanteuse blared from a fallen laptop. Right now, her feet were not bare. She wore yellow vinyl galoshes with polka dots. What a goof!

"Beatrice . . ."

"Betty."

Well, that was different. "Betty, I have Ginsberg, Genet, Goll, Goethe, Gifford . . ."

"Any of them not a white guy?" asked Betty.

"Mmm. No. A couple of them were gay, one was German . . ."

She dropped it for a moment. "Can I read a poem? Or maybe it's a song . . . It's called 'Road Song'?"

"Betty, the class would be overjoyed, I'm sure."

If there was sarcasm no one cared. She read from the notebook in front of her, something in scrawly script:

Road Song:
My mother is a golf-cart
My father is a four-wheeler
My boyfriend is a foul-mouthed driver
I'm a wheeler-dealer.
We are a family of assholes.

Great poem. Were these, I wondered, the lyrics of a pop song I didn't know because I hadn't listened to a pop song in decades, and not only wasn't I hip to what the kids were listening to, but I was reasonably sure that it was crap? My prejudice was firmly based on the occasional bit of song that floated my way from radios or patios in student apartments, or Whole Foods and Starbucks. What sound and words actually encased and isolated their young heads from the outside I did not truly know. Under the occasional public noise there was surely a more intimate layer full of meaning about life, love, and the state of the union. Like this poem. I'd been to a few bars where young bands played, but I'd always heard only the conversation, the words, either mine or somebody else's, never the music. I was fond of saying, "I hate music," but that was just pose. I love music, but not as background. I like listening, I can't do anything else when I listen. I learned this from Laura, who likes to separate firmly certain activities: listening from talking, eating from drinking, writing from listening, talking from viewing. If her attention is to a writer, she'll read every book s/he wrote and track herm down through every reference until she's drained the public record. If it's Tuscan cooking, we live with pasta and herbs until the herb garden freezes. Bluegrass, Herodotus, whiskey, poetry, you all have her full attention, one at a time, please. There is a lot of complexity in monomania.

"That's great. Can you sing that? Are you in a band?" Silly question. Of course she was. Youth now divided in two: throwbacks with bands and nerds with startups. The two were not that different: both paths, of the heart and of the brain, so to speak, aimed for love. These were love-starved kids determined to get it either by singing or by making money. But the content of their songs and the tendency of their startups was communitarian. It was an interesting time in America: our country suddenly had more singers than machinists, more waiters than carpenters, more nerds than farmers. Every part of the human body, except for the slice of brain that produced math, music, and pheromones, was banished to other countries. Labor and class became in a very short time restructured by geography instead of ability. Colonialism was back with a vengeance. And we had a few soldiers, like Hillary Adams, in case the pie got unevenly sliced.

"Yeah, we're playing at the Red Star Friday, we are The Monickers."

There it was, in a nutshell. Commie kitsch. And wordplay on "The Monkeys." In every American city of the twenty-first century there was now a hole-in-the-wall where disaffected and affluent youth sat between walls festooned with sickles-and-hammers, wearing Che Guevara™ tees, drinking mojitos and doing drugs in the unisex bathrooms. Who Karl Marx was they didn't know. Che Guevara's face™ was on everything, including panties and briefs. Wherever they looked they saw themselves reflected, their faces so young, pretty, in the hard red and black mirror of symbols empty of ideology. The chic was already worn out in most of these places, eBay was full of discount commie stuff that had already served as kitsch once and gone back in the trash heap. Bands called "The Monickers," "Working Class Heroes," "Velveteen Vampires" played on their stages, their names as nonreferential and matter-of-fact as the nonwords and nontunes, ahhh, ahhh, electronics, distortion, de-emphasis. Everybody "bound for glory," as Woodie Guthrie once had it, but what glory nobody knew. Outside the scene of ever-hopeful hipsters there simmered the world of "straight-edgers," a skinhead-styled subculture of abstinence and heroism with tints of racism and survivalist ethos, a mostly macho crowd wearing Jesus' face™ on wife-beater tees.

"I would like to assign you Allen Ginsberg, Betty, but I think that you'll become the envy of the class, an object of jealous rage."

"Why?"

"Why? Why, class?"

Matt said, "I'd rather take the Queen of Romania."

"She's all yours, Matt," I said, "I've never read her poetry myself. I think it's full of shepherds."

Bennigan said, "I prefer Charles Bukowski and Shel Silverstein."

"I *will* be jealous," said Trotsky mildly. "My mother gave me acid when I was ten and played Allen Ginsberg reading 'Kaddish.' It was an *experience*."

"I bet it was, JJ. How did you survive?"

"I'm not sure I did."

"You did," I said firmly. "If you listened to it all the way to the end where the sunlight comes in the window, you were released from hell and you are OK today."

Jason Jacob smiled. "I know, I was just checking."

"So you survived and have no need whatsoever of jealousy. In fact, you and Betty can share Allen Ginsberg."

"He was gay," said Betty, "I think he'd like Jason better."

"I don't think so, though I may be the only poet in America to hold this opinion. I think that Allen was gay because Walt Whitman might have been, because it was the American thing to do . . . He also worshipped handsome men like Jack Kerouac and Neal Cassady, and he doubtlessly enjoyed giving head, but I think that he was straight . . ."

I'm not sure that anybody, including JJ, had any idea what I was talking about. JJ had survived Allen's reading of "Kaddish" on acid, and Betty had probably had parts of "Howl" read to her by a boy who looked up from the book after every long line and stared intensely at her nipples. She ended up being so aroused by these stares following the end of Ginsberg's long Whitmanic lines, that she cut the reading short, sent the boy home, and called building maintenance to complain about the faulty heater, and then fucked the middle-aged black man with the gold tooth who came up to take a look. None of her experiences with Ginsberg so far had anything to do with homosexuality, except for remembering the way the solemn nipple-raising boy said, "I'm gonna read Ginsberg to you. He was gay."

"Professor, I read somewhere that Allen Ginsberg saw William Blake speaking to him," said Jason Jacob, "so if Blake was Ginsberg's Ghost-Companion, that would make Blake my Grand-Ghost-Companion, no?"

"Well, yes, Jason. I think that you hit on something. If every poet had a G-C, you're related to every poet when you take a G-C of your own."

"Blake, now here is one scary bloodsucker!" sneered Matt Borden. "Listen to this . . ." He read from his screen: "'*Better strangle an infant in the cradle than nurse unwanted desires.*' Man, that would make a hell of a *CSI*. Mother kills the baby and says William Blake made her do it. Whispered in her ear, 'Strangle that baby . . . 'cause you can't go out.'"

Smart cookie, the milkman. "How about 'The road of excess leads to the palace of wisdom'?" I said. I'd quoted this Blake maxim often over the years, to give my own road of excess poetic credibility.

"I don't like drugs," Borden said flatly, "if that's what it takes to get to the palace of wisdom, I'll stay on the farm." A mother's joy, this Matthew. A few decades back a maniac had struck at the heart of the American family by poisoning a Tylenol bottle. It was like an attack on milk, and it may have been the deciding moment in the Borden family when horror of drugs along with distaste for the prophetic mode entered their bloodstream.

A good thing, probably. The messianic industry was a strange tangle of excessive roads, to be sure. Prophets were tireless and scary. I thought of Allen Ginsberg working all the time, camera in hand, dragging heavy bags full of books from airport to airport and up to guru caves looking for the big OK, and then OK or no, playing sage of rock 'n' roll, king of the underground, antiwar chief, voice for legal pot and psychedelics, importer of Buddhism and Hare Krishna to America, gay liberator, member of the Mattachine and the Man-Boy Love Society. Blake, Whitman, Ginsberg, all possessed G-Cs of each other's big agendas of universal and androgynous freedom, stopped by no articulate power except perverse and inarticulate reality. I know, because for most of our revolution, when Ginsberg was king, we said one thing but did another. Contradiction may be human, as Whitman said, but living constantly with it was kind of tense. The androgynous hairy species to which I once tenuously belonged was sexy only to very young women who found androgyny less threatening than soldierly straighforwardness. When they were no longer afraid, by age 23, let's say, they preferred men with muscles and very hard cocks with an uncomplicated (they hoped) view of the world. Later, they married rich guys and fucked juniors. All of this was culturally *verboten* for most of the Seventies, when heterosexuality, marriage, and all the negative emotional baggage those two carried became philosophically suspect. That sliver of cultural difference born in a suspended moment of visionary hubris was fertile enough to give birth to dissertations and university courses in "Queer Studies," establish hundreds of ashrams, attract followers to mass-suicide cults and Scientology, and allow extraterrestrials free access to the planet, where they are to this day conducting their experiments on us through Hollywood film. I was alive when vision became professional, children, and what a time it was! Now the Beats have turned into books, lots of them. Being "gay" is mostly theoretical, and so evident to many young women scholars of Queer Studies that they didn't even notice the widening gap between theory and practice, as they got married, had children, and began shopping and joining health clubs. Everything happens fast and everything happened a long time ago, or else nothing happens but the endless production of nonsense. On the floor above the one where I was tormenting poets, tenured professors tapped steadily on their keyboards, completely uninterested in the deep ravine that ran between their professional thoughts and their lives. No wonder that the young mocked (or would have liked to) everything that was glaringly hypocritical in their elders. It had always been thus, but it was worse, I think, now, when every proof for one thing or another is intellectually available, but tips and hints on how to really live are rarer than asparagus stalks in Eskimo cuisine. And never in the history of the world had we a more prosperous commerce in "how to live" manuals, television channels, and spiritual disciplines. The menu is immense. A young person looking at the cornucopia has little choice but to faint, vomit, or over-dose, though even that had been done by the punks and duly marketed.

"I don't envy you, any of you. Take Ginsberg, Betty, download 'Kaddish' and invite Jason over to your place so you can listen together. He already has an insight and you'll share Ginsberg together. Allen liked threesomes. And orgies. He was actually pansexual. And with all the G-Cs it will be a regular bacchanal."

The prospect of sharing the nipple-arousing poet and bringing back a ten-year-old's acid experience and hippie up-bringing was irresistible. Heat rose and was felt by all, and one more pair was bonded by a poet. I am great. The *shadchen* of American poetry. I'd considered at some point making "Shadchen" my middle name. I'd matched many people in many countries, and on two continents. In some cases, I'm proud to say, I took my pay in advance and then acciden-tally, only accidentally, paired an intended to a destined one. Now I'd gone over the edge and I was also pairing the living with the dead. It's the kind of thing you can do when you're about to retire.

"Let's not go there," said Betty. "I'm a cultural lesbian."

Yes, I knew that. Cultural lesbians had blown through my classes like the mistral.

They had been born in required classes in feminist theory, taught by assistant professors from Vassar, who authorized what the girls already knew was the best course of study: sleeping with a girl until graduation. Very few real lesbians came out of these liaisons. Half the couple got married to a man shortly after graduation, leaving her girlfriend's heart in tatters. Some of the brokenhearted GF's may have gone on to play for the gay team, but I wonder how many of yesteryear's cultural lesbians still practice the sapphic arts. Readers, can we have a show of hands, please?

"Fine then, have Gabriela Mistral for a G-C. The last letter of her name does not start with the last letter of yours, but it's a *cultural* match."

"Who's that?" Betty was suspicious.

"Chilean love and nature poet, won the Nobel Prize early in the twentieth century. A cultural lesbian. Totally. But if you change your mind by next class, let us know. Jason, what think you?" Jason feigned indifference, which is about the only thing the young are *very* good at. Ours is not a heroic age and it embarrasses them. They prefer doom to nothingness, but there it is: if you can't have doom, feign indifference. I don't believe that indifference exists in humans between ages six months and eighty-eight years old. Interest varies with mood, of course, but no one is indifferent to being directly addressed. People react more emotionally to being adored or insulted, but a Ghost-Companion does not leave them indifferent, either. Young Trotsky felt rejected. He slung a brief steel-tipped arrow at his future girlfriend, Betty, who looked unaware of the wound.

"Moving on. Beatrice Garland, take Gabriela Mistral. Be happy. Mr. Ferris . . ."

"Present. I'm an economics major with a Pell grant, I don't know anything about poetry. I took this class for my requirement, so I don't know where I'm going to find the money for anything in this class. How much does a goatskin notebook cost? I don't even know what anybody's talking about."

"It's a giveaway of poets, Mr. Ferris. This English requirement is an introduction to poetry writing . . . so I'm giving away a poet to each of you so that you might take her or him as a guide, to study, learn from, and enter into psychic communication with. I found it nearly impossible in all my years of teaching to induce poetry in someone without the help of another poet . . . it's like lifting a very heavy object . . . you need two people. Some of my students have gone on and kept their poet long past graduation. A former student, now an advertising executive in Denver, writes to me that whenever he has a difficult campaign he calls on Pablo Neruda. Invariably he gets his answer. A senior editor at a big New York publisher has changed her last name to Myles, in honor of the poet Eileen Myles, who she now carries on her driver's license, not just in her heart. One of my students is the founder of a billion-dollar Internet startup called Dante, who was his first G-C, but he has, unfortunately, registered every poet he could think of as his domain name. He's got Villon.com and Homer.com, and I'm in a big fight with him right now because I think that's unethical and, well, insane. He's even grabbed living poets without websites and practically owns them. He won't even sell them back their own names because he's under the delusion that they are all his G-Cs now. That's crazy, people. One G-C is sometimes too much for a person, but two! Think of what the inside of your head might sound like if you asked the Roman poet Ovid and the French poet Antonin Artaud to tell you what to have for dinner! GOAT BALLS IN ASPIC! QUAIL EGGS IN BRAIN SAUCE! And it doesn't stop there, though this dude is the most egregious case of G-C nymphomania I can think of. A now very famous TV writer who sat at the back of the class and chewed gum has written a best-selling book called *The Story of Stories*, about daytime soaps, under a pseudonym that combined his last name, Godfrey, with the poet Dave Brinks's, making Godfrey Brinks a rich man. This book by Godfrey Brinks is 7,900 pages long and weighs 89 pounds, it can only be lifted by two people, and, because of its folio size, it must also be read by two people, one to read and one to turn the pages. So you, see, Mr. Ferris, this is an object that was literally created by a student not only through spiritual but through *material*, seriously material, bonding with a G-C. The price of a goatskin notebook is small potatoes compared to the benefits you'll derive from acquiring a Ghost-Companion."

I paused. I always pause after a speech like that. In the old days, I used to light a cigarette and let out a long sigh of satisfaction and a ring of smoke. These aren't the old days. Are these even "days" anymore? It's not easy living in the future, let me tell you.

Betty interrupted my transfer of a poet to John Ferris. "If I change my mind and do Ginsberg, after all, can I have Mistral, too?"

I looked at Jason Jacob. "The more the merrier?"

Jason had a flashback. The living room of the communal house in the redwoods in northern California. The smell of brown rice and soy sauce, the pitty-patter of naked feet on a frosty morning, mommy sleeping in a pile of nude communards, some of them snoring, like a many-headed octopus of love and bad breath. An equally spent incense holder and an ashtray smoldered on a Moroccan brass table. Surrounding the sleeping multi-eyed octopus were several cats, gracefully alone in their feline depths. Jason's task was to find a part of his mother, preferably a hand, to pull on, for the purposes of getting her to make him oatmeal. After a thorough look at the many Indian toe-rings, silver ankle bracelets, Sanskrit tattoos, and curls of head and pubic hair, black, grey, ash-blonde, and red, or maybe even purple, Jason recognized his mommy's wrist, even as her hand slept gripping his "uncle" Gandalf's ankle. Jason took hold and pulled: mommy moved and the people-mound shifted, sighed, tightened its grip on itself, and slept again. Jason pulled harder. After a long time, during which Jason pulled and pulled, mommy stretched and wiggled and extricated her short, muscular, large-breasted body from the LG (Loving Group) or MCF (Mongolian Cluster Fuck) and rose to boil Jason's oatmeal. She was still sleepy, naked, and cold, so Jason brought her his Star Wars blanket to wrap around herself. What beautiful, luxurious black pubic hair mommy had! She put on Jason's blanket and didn't wake until she burned herself trying to light the fire in the wood stove. "Fucking goddam, Jason!" she cried, "You're old enough to make your own fucking breakfast!" She sucked on the burn on her hand and caressed the top of his head with her unburnt hand. Jason wanted to kiss mommy's booboo to make it better, but the communards were beginning to wake up, and soon the sounds of "Stairway to Heaven" drowned the house in familiarity.

"You better be sure of this, Miss Garland, because as in the cautionary tale I just told, two G-Cs can cause mental disequilibrium. Poets don't much care for other poets, though most of them associate with poets. Many poets can be seen drinking and arguing or agreeing with other poets, but secretly, or not so secretly, everyone thinks that he or she is the better, perhaps the *only* poet. Poets in their youth begin in gangs, but as they age they seek asylum in small towns. Allen Ginsberg and Gabriela Mistral are from different eras and from different bardic traditions, but who knows? In the other world, which is just like ours only more logical, they might be great friends. The poet James Merrill was asked by the *Paris Review* to interview the dead poet William Carlos Williams by means of the Ouija board that Merrill used to obtain his own poems from. Merrill Ouija-phoned the dead Williams and obtained a detailed description of the various associations that had sprung up in the beyond. He found from Williams, who spoke in metered free verse, that the nether world had many rooms, but that the two major groups there had two large clubhouses, one for *gay poets* and one for *straight poets*. The gay poets' club was led by Gertrude Stein, and a lot more fun was to be had there. The other, led by Doc Williams, was straitlaced, angry, and humorless. I was amused when I read that interview in the *Paris Review*, but I didn't believe a word of it. James Merrill has since passed on, so he's doubtlessly in a better position to know if he was *actually* hearing Williams or just *imagining* it. Now, if you are dedicated to having two G-Cs, Miss Garland, you are certainly welcome to use my very own Ouija board to interview James Merrill as to the state of relations between Ginsberg and Mistral . . . that is, before you commit."

I no longer possess a Ouija board. Are they still made and sold? A clumsy board with letters and numbers, it was invented in World War One for mothers to communicate with their dead sons. Messages of love and sorrow went back and forth until the war ended, but the popularity of the dead remained because the living still sought information. In the late 1960s, the hippies brought back the Ouija and it became everybody's favorite party game as angels with names like Ariel and Isistra brought good news of the Age of Aquarius. Then, inexplicably, the good-news angels vanished, and in their stead came demons named Azrael and Beelzebub bearing dark news that freaked everybody out. The end was near. Black panthers prowled the streets. There were guts in the soup, snakes in the hair. The Ouija got put away. I simply lost mine, during one of the many zigs and zags I made between cities and countries in the next decade. Merrill and his boyfriend kept theirs and used it like a fast typing machine,

63

a pre-computer, really. Their prodigious output was aston-
ishing to me because even in my Ouijiest days I'd never gotten more than a few cryptic syllables out of the device. Most
people just got a Yes or No, which were writ large at the top
of the board. For that reason I rarely asked questions that
required more than a yes or no answer. So if Beatrice, Betty,
really took me up on it, I'd have to either dive into a past
attic or go on eBay for a Ouija.

Happily, she didn't. "I'll take them both, professor. I don't
need a Ouija board to know which way the wind blows."
Clever bugger. There are way too many movies about my
life.

After distributing Ginsberg and Mistral, I decided to give
them a break. "Take five minutes, class. Five minutes, I said.
No more no less. I know what a minute is. A New York minute. Take five New York minutes."

I watched them scatter like bladders with legs out the
door. Two hours, two breaks, and they felt like eternity. Intro
to Poetry Writing is always like this: a long labor, a breech
birth, or, obversely, mining in the dark. You take healthy
young Americans used to sunshine (aided sometimes by
Xanax and Adderall), you blindfold them and lead them by
the hand into a labyrinth made from bones. Then you tell
them their assignment: "Find the Grail. You have a New
York minute to get it."

And then came that saddest of all moments in the life of a
teacher, when he sits at his desk alone, in a classroom still
redolent of the young unwashed, empty and quiet. Thus they
have gone, year after year, break after break, flocks of uncer-
tain humans headed for the unpredictable, the unexpected,
the unimaginable. Or obversely, for the predictable, the ex-

pected, and the easily imaginable. It occurred to me, at the very beginning of this fraudulent enterprise, that these creatures had mothers and fathers and had come from histories as deep or as wide as their roots, and that some of them already had histories themselves. It seemed to me that American kids were younger than European kids, or at least I was older when I was their age. But then, the right to a prolonged childhood was hard fought-for and laboriously won by generation after generation, wherever and whenever. The long, physical strain of standing and fighting only to earn the right to lie down and dream was humanity's story. Americans had won the right to the thirty-year childhood through exhausting effort and great ingenuity. The Protestant ethic of "hard work" that was instilled in the original American strain was for the purpose of the next generation achieving childhood, a "utopia." Seen this way, my labors were not in vain. I taught them to disregard everything that was boring. They were my allies now because as long as they remained children their gestures were still new, they were still imbued with freshness, the milk of beginning still clung to them like snot from baby noses. The most sensitive ones sensed the coming of mind-numbing repetition and of being cornered, so they tried their best to stay new, to the point, sometimes, of killing themselves. Of my four suicides over a quarter century of teaching, only one succeeded. The rest failed from clumsiness or because they waited too long for someone to see them dying. The someone never showed, but a passerby, an accidental witness, showed up and saved them. A brilliant sonnetist wrote with menstrual blood on the door of my office, "I'm waiting for you for one day." That was one day too long for me. I was out of my office that week. Her father, a brilliant math professor, came by to see me on a matter concerning her sonnets and recognized her handwriting on the door. He had her hospitalized, pills pumped out, then stabilized with Prozac and some other pills. Shortly after, she abandoned the sonnet and married a silent Jewish philosopher for whom she abandoned Catholicism also, though she sang so beautifully at her conversion ceremony, her voice could have only been forged in a musically alert church. Jews don't sing like that. She produced three children, taught Jewish Sunday school, and became the author of noted articles on child-rearing. I'd say that she was a success, a triumph of transference, who had nearly died for her right to remain a child, but transitioned well to becoming an expert on the subject instead. She championed childhood with the fervor of Emma Goldman (who she ended up resembling) championing feminism. In other words, she became a good American. My other two failures at suicide ended up in the computer industry. The more brilliant of the two sabotaged a widely distributed video game by burying in its deepest recesses a reward that consisted of two boys sucking each other's cocks. Only the most sophisticated players of the game could reach that level, but one of these turned out to be his boss, who discovered the two young homosexuals and fired the saboteur on the spot. One hundred thousand copies of the game had already been shipped, and every single one had to be recalled. My poet became an instant hero to the hacker underground and won an important monetary reward from an anonymous (and rich) source, which enabled him to change his identity and go on to become the creator of mirror websites that brought down several major businesses and government offices, and threatened world security. Today, he is one of the most wanted men in the world and the subject of numerous *techno-corridos* that lionize him. From a child and a would-be suicide, my pupil transitioned most successfully to becoming the nemesis of the corporate world, its dark-side mirror-image, a black hole that generates poetry and song. My third suicide had come to me empty inside, a beautiful California surfer boy whose interior had been bleached by the sun, absent parents, and an abundance of toys. He had been vampirized by an absence so profound, I inherited only a shell on an expensive motorcycle who was dragged from bed to bed by every one of his classmates, each abandoning him after one night, terrified at the hollowness they'd elicited. I tried finding some resonance. I hit him like a hidden gong with my boot. I tied him up and played Pound in his ears for a whole month, but nothing could be heard over the surf of the Pacific and the vrrrooom of his BMW. He drove his motorcycle off a mountainside in Kentucky, but a pine branch caught him and held him there until an insurance company came to get him. He now sells real estate in Nevada on the Internet and has regularly scheduled surgeries that will enable him to live five hundred years. His name is The Future. My only successful suicide was a boy who so loved poetry he traveled to every library within his budget, beginning with our very own university library, and circled the word "one" or the number "1" in every poetry book in the collection. That was fifteen years ago, and to this day my students take poetry books out of the library and find "one" and "1" circled everywhere they occur. Most libraries do not find it worth replacing their entire poetry collections because of the circled number, so my student's work will survive to the end of time. Or to the end of libraries. It is a difficult estimate, but I believe that he has left his mark in over a million books. He hit all the major university libraries, including the Harvard Poetry Collection and the Library of Congress. He did not care if he worked over the same book, as long as it was poetry and its "one"s or "1"s were pristine. I can't decide if his action was a way of affirming uniqueness, his own or the poets', by claiming "I am one, or 1," or whether it was an ironic commentary on the cult of the individual that poetry, unfortunately, fosters. Was my suicide a panegyrist or an ironist? I tend to think that he was the latter, because panegyrists do not kill themselves. Do ironists? Hard to say, but judging by the only study I have made, more ironists jump off the Golden Gate Bridge into the Bay facing the city of San Francisco, than panegyrists who leap into the unknown Ocean and its vast nothingness. It has been speculated (by my dear poet-friends over many whiskies) that the Ocean-leapers gave a shout of joy, "Yippee!," when they hurled themselves into the great beyond, while the ironists looked with melancholy at the city that had rejected them, and murmured (ironically), "You'll miss me, bitch!"

"Yippee!" is a *panegyric*. "You'll miss me, bitch!" is *bitter irony*.

My students started returning, one by one, ounces of urine lighter. Some were even smiling, as if the brief contact with their genitals had restored their sense of well-being. Yes, I know. Assignments can be a downer. But I was not done assigning. Last semester I'd assigned "sadomasochism and creative misreading," and now there were ghosts to distribute and many lines to scan before the end of class.

John "call me 'Jack'" Ferris still smelled like smoke. He'd had another during break, perhaps even peed while smoking. He did look like young Johnny Rotten, years away from coherence. An economics major? More like a burglar pretending to be a ballerina.

"Doctor, I googled Ferlinghetti and it'll soon be time to get out of here. I want Ferlinghetti." He said this before he even sat down, which prompted Bennigan to quip, "We do have to get out of here no matter who Ferlinghetti is!"

I had nothing against assigning the great poet-citizen, San Francisco's anarchist Charlie Chaplin who named his bookstore City Lights and published the Beats, to Jack Ferris, but I wasn't going to make it easy. I spent an entire night in the early Eighties arguing with Ted Berrigan and Anselm Hollo *for* Ferlinghetti's poetry. That was two of them (Ted and Anselm) against one (me). Granted, we stayed up all night many nights in those days, drinking and doing bumps now and then, so this kind of debate was not unheard of, it was almost a game. This particular argument, however, was quite sharp, and it had a depth that became downright personal and offensive at times, and at one point it looked like a physical fight might break out, which was nothing short of ridiculous because poets are lousy fighters. Besides, we were at my house in Baltimore and my wife and child were sleeping, and if we'd fallen over the furniture, she'd have come down and kicked *all* our asses. I have no idea what it was about Ferlinghetti's poetry that aroused such passions. Everyone agreed that the man was exceptional, a person of integrity and conviction; a wonderful publisher, a tolerant bookstore owner where in my youth I often stole my first book to give to girls who waited outside in the rain for me to see if I really was who I said I was, a published poet, and seeing (from the first poem they read) that I really was, slept with me at the $5-a-night Dante Hotel; an anarchist and pacifist resister in World War Two; a civic activist who persuaded the city of San Francisco to name numerous streets after poets and writers; a partisan of our art; and an upright human being who spoke at public meetings. His poetry, however, was a battlefield. I stood sword and shield on the side of Ferlinghetti, who wrote the poetry best seller (an unequalled feat)

A *Coney Island of the Mind*, while Ted sent his formidable armies against us. Anselm, who tended in those days to agree with everyone who bought the next drink, campaigned first with me, then with Ted, in whose camp he faithfully stayed until dawn came and he passed out. Poetry is a bloody business and it's for no idle reason that Sultan Murat the Second demanded his battlefield dispatches in verse and beheaded unskilled generals. After Anselm passed out and a huge red sun rose over the red brick of Baltimore's row houses, Ted and I kept skirmishing over the merits of Ferlinghetti's poetry, a battle that by that time was no longer about Ferlinghetti's poetry at all, but poetry and the polis, the agora and the poet; in my view all poetry was political because it critiqued intrinsically all that came before it, including poetry, and Ted thought it something deliberate, an effort like getting out of bed to go to a meeting and fight the police, and so we shouted until my wife woke up, and then it was over, her dreams had been troubled. We took my five-year-old son to the Inner Harbor, where we walked in the chilly morning, and continued to argue, as the little fellow tried to keep up with the chain-smoking fiends, one of whom was his delirious father. He tugged at my shirt as we went past a diner and said, "I'm thirsty!" I didn't hear him and I said, "It's part of who the citizen is!," and Ted said, "for chrissakes!," and steered the kid into the diner and asked for a glass of water. I was stunned by the extraordinary speed of change in Ted's priorities, and his marvelous response won him the argument. In the end, Ferlinghetti had nothing to do with it. A responsible citizen of the world sees to it first that children get water when they are thirsty. Ted dropped the jive at the first sound of real human need and *acted*. Poetry schmoetry. Ted was my hero, and today he's my G-C. Today, I'll get you a glass of water if you're thirsty, even if it means delaying my

Nobel Prize by thirty years. A lesson like that you don't get in school. I was reluctant to hand Ferlinghetti over to Jack Ferris, my business major, for fear that he might employ him to manipulate the stock market somehow. On the other hand, Ferlinghetti, publisher and store owner, was no slouch at business. I knew he'd do Ferris good: for one thing, the boy had googled him, more than you can say for the English majors who were either slam-frequenters or fresh from the fields. It also looked like Ferris needed to quit smoking, and if ever there was a foe of that habit, it was San Francisco's poet laureate.

So I said, "You can't just *have* Ferlinghetti. You have to *memorize* him!"

"That's not why I'm saying it, man! I mean, you better give him to me now, we have to hurry up." Ferris looked grave.

I looked around and saw that everyone's smiles had vanished.

Chloe looked at her cell phone screen like she'd just seen Death.

"What is it?"

"Text-message alert," said Chloe.

"It's just an alert, man," said Betty Garland.

I was at a crossroads again. This seems to occur with some regularity these days. I don't mean the ever-present crossroads that face one every second: do I turn left or right? Do I go or do I stay? Those are fundamental. My successful suicide had glimpsed fundamental binary nature and made a choice: "one" or "1." Had he continued to oscillate, as we all must, between "1" and "0" he'd have had no reason to off himself. We live with the paradox and the choices of our binary reality because, as Ted once put it, "the job of the organism is to survive." The kind of crossroads I was at now was of the sort that occurs more often these days, like torna-does, earthquakes, floods, holes in the ozone, falling satel-lites, terror alerts, financial crises of a magnitude inconceiv-able hitherto. At the first sight of such incoming horrors, the roads divide quickly, sometimes leaving a person only a few minutes to make a choice between running left or right, up-stairs or downstairs, outside or inside. This particular cross-roads was caused by a text message I hadn't yet read, but that clearly scared my students enough to make them unsure of whether they would stay or go.

"What does the test alert say?"

Betty read: "'This is a test of the university-wide text-mes-sage alert. If you have received it, you will be alerted in an emergency, and told where to take shelter and find safety. This is only a test, so if you are reading it, the test was suc-cessful.'"

"So, it's only a test. What's the problem?"

"Yeah," said Bennigan, "we're students. We live for tests."

"The problem is the language," exclaimed Chloe. "I want to find safety *now*. I want my hammock! I feel threatened. Boo-hoo!" She made a cry-face. "I don't like being nervous every time I look at my cell phone. I have lots of people tex-ting me. Now I'll think every text is a threat."

Jason Jacob said calmly, "One out of every two people in the United States has a handgun. One in three people is being treated for depression. Ninety percent of all people are ca-pable of killing other people, and will, if threatened. Seventy-five percent of the students on this campus come from single-parent families. One person in a million, Zed Bennigan, owns an empty intercontinental ballistic missile silo. He is in this class. What are the odds that a psycho with a handgun is also in this class, ready to trigger a *real* alert?" He leaned back and grinned.

"What?" My economics major was properly stunned. Maybe poetry and class and Ferlinghetti weren't for him. There was still time to drop out.

Nor did the rest look reassured.

This was a crossroads that called for poetry. This crossroads was not entirely my students' problem, though it clearly concerned them; this was a narrative crossroads. I've sworn off postmodern cheap tricks in this story, but this one can't be helped. It's a crossroads in a story. If I take the road to the left, there will be no sudden dramatic development. My students will sit down and I will continue in the pedagogical-memorialistic mode that has so far held your attention, reader (because if it hadn't you wouldn't have gotten this far). My students will sit down; I will continue assigning them poets whose last names begin with the same letters as theirs; I'll continue to give them complex assignments that will culminate (I'm giving away some of the future delights, but they may be feints) in a fashion show à la *Project Runway* called *Poetry Runway*, where, using their G-Cs, the protopoets of Intro will create paper dresses and costumes covered with the words of the greats, among which they might include their own (I'm closing my eyes), at a Facebook-advertised public performance in Free Speech Alley; a sudden torrential tropical rain will shred the paper clothes, or if no rain (a regular afternoon event at the end of August) we will produce the torrent ourselves with the aid of guerrilla hosers. Like I said, I'm not saying that this is what is actually going to happen, or that this is what happened, but it is certain that if I go to the left in this story, the *Poetry Runway* is *sure* to happen. If I take the road to the right, something dramatic, momentous, horrible, tragic will take place: a bombing, a maniac with grenades, a terrorist attack, the assassination of the President, an earthquake—in short, one of

73

those things we have been conditioned by media to believe are *natural*. Nature itself has nothing to say in this matter because the battle between nature and virtuality has long ago been won by virtuality. If something horrible and naturally consequential happens, then every person in class will have to reveal herm character during the mayhem to follow, becoming in the process a *real character*. Which is the road I'd be forced to take if this was, let's say, *a novel*. This is not a novel, but then neither is it poetry, because if this story were poetry I'd take the road to the right without any qualms of the sort I'm confessing. No, this story is not a novel or poetry, and it's no essay or memoir either, though it mimics aspects of both. What happens at such crossroads is unknown because no such crossroads occur outside self-conscious postmodernism. I only know one thing for sure: in an old fairy tale two brothers come to a crossroads. One of them plants his knife into the place where the roads diverge, and tells the other, "If this knife is rusted when you pass this way again, brother, you will know that I am dead. If it is I who pass this way and find the knife rusted, I'll know that you are dead. Farewell." The brothers embrace and each brother takes a different road. The problem here is that you, my reader, are my brother. Will either one of us pass this way again? Only time will tell. I took the road to the left.

"Sit down. It's only a text-alert test on your cell phone, a sign of the times. You can no more be safe from your times than you can be from my pedagogical wrath. Mr. Ferris, you can have Ferlinghetti."

At the fiftieth anniversary of the founding of City Lights Bookstore I gave Ferlinghetti two character-engraved Japanese stones. One of them said "Longevity," the other, "Compassion." Lawrence rolled them around, feeling the texture, then handed me back "Longevity." "You need this one more than me, I'm already ninety. But this 'Compassion,' OK, I'll keep it, Allen always talked about it, but I never figured out what he meant."

I laughed because I thought that he was being funny, but then I thought about it too, and I couldn't figure out what "compassion" was, either. I knew that it was one of the basic precepts of Buddhism that Allen Ginsberg talked about a lot. I had never figured out how "compassion" worked with "detachment," which was another Buddhist precept of equal value. "Detachment" seemed somehow the opposite of "compassion," even if it just meant serenity. I could easily see my serene detachment dissolved like sugar in hot tea by a sudden onrush of compassion. Compassion, in the sense of feeling like hugging a widow at graveside, contains no detachment, as far as I can see. Worse, it can lead to an erection, which, in its own clumsy way, is the opposite of detachment. An erection has no other purpose than to attach itself to a human being for whom one feels (hopefully) compassion. What's more, an erection that feels no compassion for a human being to whom it points, accidentally perhaps, might acquire some if the human in question welcomes it. In either case, no detachment is involved.

Ferlinghetti had other unorthodox ideas about the Beat Generation™. He pshawed the label. "The whole Beat thing was just Allen's P.R. genius." And that was true, if one looked at the many poets who bummed drinks and smoke under the umbrella of said "Beat Generation." It was clever branding, but it wasn't all P.R. No matter what different types hung out at the Beat Cafe or shot up heroin and speed, aka goofballs, at the Beat Hotel, or how many bad movies and kitsch were produced under the label, the fact remains that both "Beat" and "Generation" stand for something inexpressible, and in combination express something expressible in no other way. "Beat" by itself describes both music and being tired. In combination with any number of prepositions it covers a large field; it's both a noun and an adverb, and it morphs into the verb Michael Jackson turned into "Beat it!" As for the idea of a "generation" distinct from all others, once it had been theorized by Ortega y Gasset it became commonplace, though no one can agree how long a generation is, not even lab scientists who see "generations" of flies come and go faster than any historian. The word has grave built-in resonance, the resonance of the grave, it sets into motion the whole delicate machinery of mortality, or at least one's received ideas of it. "Generation" boings like a gong *de profundis* in the mind. The power of the two words, "beat" and "generation," rests in the impossibility of describing precisely what they mean, yet feeling deeply their touch and, believing, for a second, that you actually *know* what they mean. You don't: I have it from Ferlinghetti.

"And once you memorize *A Coney Island of the Mind*, Mr. Ferris, I'd like you to perform the following exercise for one week: you will rise at 9 a.m . . ." Class laughter, Zed Bennigan, mumble, mumble, ". . . at 9 a.m., or earlier if the class keeps guffawing, and after writing down your dreams and composing your daily epitogram in your goatskin notebook, you will pretend to be an old man."

"Pretend to be an old man?" Ferris didn't understand.

"A vigorous old man, Ferris. A tall, athletic nonagenarian, who takes his dog for a walk, enjoying the brisk air of morning in San Francisco . . ."

"In Louisiana?" Bennigan couldn't help himself.

"Well, you are *pretending* to be an old man," I said, resorting to my pedagogical mode, "so why can you not *pretend* that you're in brisk *San Francisco* instead of humid sweaty *Louisiana*?"

Bennigan said, "Then why not *pretend* it's 9 a.m., even if it's actually 3 p.m., when I'd *prefer* to get up . . ."

"Because, Mr. Bennigan, in the course of an assignment, the assignee can only *pretend* as many times as the exercise *requires*, and that's only twice." I turned back to Ferris, hoping that Borden, who seemed way too well-read for an Introduction to Poetry Writing student, wouldn't also call my bluff by questioning my authority. An exercise of the sort I was proposing would only work if there was authority involved, an assignator and an assignee, not some sort of dissolved narrator! Blissfully, Borden looked asleep. Perhaps he was contemplating his imminent call to dad, to ask for an empty missile silo to bury poets in. ". . . You will walk your dog then, a terrier, in the brisk Frisco morning, toward your favorite coffeehouse in North Beach, where you will have a cappuccino and read the *San Francisco Chronicle*, mumbling indignantly under your breath about fresh injustice in the world. You will then return to your apartment with a view of the sparkling Bay and its gaily bobbing sailboats, where, shortly after you have had a breakfast of poached egg, half an English muffin, and a raw carrot, with a glass of freshly squeezed orange juice, you will get up to answer a knock at the door. Standing there in a rain slicker, as if to protect herself from the dew, is a smiling young woman. She is fresher than your orange juice this morning, a form bursting with sunshine and joy whom the hands of the boy in love who had roamed all over her the night before had left miraculously untouched, reminding you of a line of poetry by Guillevic: '*to do to things / what light does to them.*' In other words, everything and nothing. Anyway, there she is, smiling in front of you, shaking her head as if trying to get water out of her hair, and shedding, by the same motion, her rain slicker, to stand before you naked and smooth. You go to your kitchen table where your sketchbook has been waiting since last night, clear the dish and the glass, and start to sketch her."

"I can get behind that," said Ferris, with some wonder.

"Ah yes, Mr. Ferris, you like the exercise now. I see also that I have everyone's attention. Let me enjoy this for a minute."

I closed my eyes and linked my hands behind the back of my head. I leaned back in my chair. I had even silenced Bennigan. The women in class stood naked before the sketching old man, rid of their rain slickers, fresh like poems by children. I leaned forward abruptly. Better not push my luck.

"When you are done sketching your model, you pay her the modeling fee in cash, fifteen dollars an hour, I believe. She has posed for one hour. After she leaves, you pull on a Norwegian wool sweater, take a walking stick with a compass in the knob off the hook on the back of the door, and stroll back to the street, walking toward City Lights Bookstore. You climb the stairs to your office and look down on the waves of restless browsers, many of them young readers looking for books about the Beat Generation in the bookstore where the Beat Generation is sold. You sigh and pour yourself a glass of the Sonoma County zinfandel you get ten cases of every year from a lover of your poetry. You sip your wine slowly, studying a young woman in a rain slicker who seems busy stuffing books under her coat, and you wonder how she could possibly hold those books there, since you know better than anyone that she wears nothing under the coat. Wonders will never cease, you tell yourself. Is this 'compassion'? It is. And you, Ferris, are Lawrence Ferlinghetti. Please report to me in one week as to the progress of the exercise, and don't hesitate to see me during office hours, Tuesday and Thursday, noon until three p.m., if you have any difficulty."

I could see that Ferris was pondering the problem of his model, because none of the women in class was looking at him. He rather fancied, I thought, Miss Anita Washington, toward whom he'd already directed a number of glances.

"What is important is that she wear the rain slicker and nothing else," I warned Ferris. Once that had been clarified, a sensuous sigh escaped Ferlinghetti's newly minted clone. I was certain that he'd ask Miss Washington out for beer, and discuss with her the weirdness of the teacher, before getting drunk to ask what if. She'd say no.

The thing about Ferris and Ferlinghetti is the problem of swallowing something much bigger than your mouth: the trick is to squeeze like a serpent and ingurgitate slowly until you are ready to burst, full of a creature much larger than yourself. Everyone has serpent moves, especially flexible young people, so I wasn't worried about whether a twenty-something American could take in Anna Akhmatova or Ginsberg or Ferlinghetti or any of the famous poets who'd spent their lives writing and living their art. I was concerned, however, with the question of whether it was *necessary* for my students to do this. If I'd been them, I'd have flatly refused, recognizing a trap. I mean, why should a thriving young organism capable of great feats in bed and on the gym floor take on the fin-de-siècle depression or gloomy prophetic powers of any poet? Here was a mystery that couldn't simply be gotten around by saying, "because they are students and I'm the teacher!"

I went to the San Francisco airport with Lawrence Ferlinghetti in the late 1970s to welcome the Russian poet Andrei Voznesenski, who was making his first *official* tour of the United States. Voznesenski got off at the gate, looking like he'd been pickled in vodka and bitten by feral groupies. He was dragging behind him a huge leather case, a kind of oversized doctor's bag that I immediately offered to carry for him. He looked grateful and I instantly saw why: the bag weighed two tons. It was the heaviest bag I had ever lifted. "What in the world is in here?" I asked. "Keys," the poet said, "Keys to American cities. I've been to twenty-six cities and all the mayors gave me keys. Let me show . . ." The poet dropped to his knees and unclasped the monster. He pulled out a giant bronze key from a glinting pile of metal inside. "This one opens Philadelphia!" he said. It was difficult to imagine what in Philadelphia such a large key might conceivably open. Nor was the bag's weight about to decrease. We took the poet from the airport to his first appointment, with Mayor Moscone at City Hall. The Mayor, wearing a fine pair of what Ferlinghetti later called "Gucci shoes," welcomed us and said, "It is good to have a Soviet poet in San Francisco." Voznesenski mumbled "thank you," but Ferlinghetti said sharply, "Andrei's been here before, he opened for the Grateful Dead at the Fillmore. But that visit was *unofficial*." Always ready to set the record straight on behalf of what was called in those days "the counterculture," Ferlinghetti enjoyed straightening out the straights on what and who came first. The Mayor smiled and handed Andrei Voznesenski an immense iron key that he claimed was a replica of the key to the door of the church at Mission Dolores, the oldest settlement in San Francisco. The key weighed twice as much as the key to Philadelphia. I didn't ask why on God's earth the replica had to be one hundred times larger and heavier than the original. I didn't ask because I understood instinctively something about the nature of authority:

the mayor of the small city (then) of San Francisco was handing the poet visiting *officially* from Moscow, a very big city, a symbolic vision of San Francisco's (yet-unrealized) future bigness. "We are but a small Moscow now," the key said, but in the future, given our roots in religion and conquest, we'll be as big as you. Lawrence Ferlinghetti, the unofficial mayor of the San Francisco underground, established his own authority by emphasizing the historical priority of the anarchic citizenry. Both of them were handing the Russian poet a key: Ferlinghetti's key was called "hipness"; it was invisible and much easier to carry, but also a blow for democracy and the grassroots. Hipness weighed nothing and left the poet's hands free to roam around in the air or embrace somebody. The official key was a burden. A week later, Mayor Moscone was assassinated, along with City Supervisor Harvey Milk, by a disgruntled former city supervisor who believed that Moscone and Milk were handing the city over to gays and hippies. If I'd been Voznesenski, I'd have gotten rid of the back-breaking bag, or donated the keys to a smelter, but Voznesenski dutifully dragged the keys to American cities back to the USSR, to be deposited in a good-will museum, or wherever it was the Soviets stored these tokens of pomp. Voznesenski was a man with feet in two worlds: one in hipness and one in cement. Just like a student. I kind of saw my distribution of old poets to young students the same way: I was handing them heavy keys to carry around and see what they did with them. I am perverse. No getting around that. I must soon meditate on Compassion.

And you can scratch the snake metaphor. Gertrude "Trudy" Helmick was, just like her name, sturdy. She hadn't said a word for the two hours and twenty minutes since class began. She alone, in her long blue cotton dress with little flowers on it, looked capable of taking a world-famous poet within her body and making him disappear. Very little of her own body was visible, except her round face and her corn-flower blues. The white socks that rose from her shiny sensible shoes vanished into the dress that ended in a white lace collar. Was she Mormon, Old Mennonite, or Russian Old-Style Orthodox? She could have been any of those things, far from home, exiled among these corrupt tropical children, a saint among us.

"Ms. Helmick, do you have a preference? Heinrich Heine, Lyn Hejinian, Holbein, Nazim Hikmet, or Miroslav Holub?" I threw Holbein in there on purpose, to see if she knew the difference.

She didn't. She shrugged her shoulders and spoke monotonously, like a medium: "I don't know any poets. I don't know any poetry. I read from the Bible and we sing from a hymnal. I'm not even from here, I'm from Indiana, but our house burned down and my father works on an oil rig in the Gulf. I want to study nursing and I need an English requirement."

She had a strange accent, something ancient, from another time and another country, something German, Dutch, maybe old English. I asked her, "I hope you don't mind, but do you belong to an old-fashioned church? I have nothing but interest and respect for peoples' beliefs, but I'd like to know if you are offended by anything so far. In poetry class we say and write some pretty rough things, and I'd hate to make you feel bad."

"Maybe I should, but I grew up on the farm and animals do more than most people think. I'm supposed to stay away from profanity, so I won't use any bad words myself, but I'm not bothered by rough talk. I think that most people are now pretty loose-lipped, sad, so I'm not sitting in judgment of anybody." She blushed.

What she said was sound, but the fact is that the temperature in class, like the temperature in most of my poetry classes, had long risen past a comfortable degree. It wasn't just Chloe in her wife-beater tee who'd thrown down her jacket. Sweat was wheeling under everyone's arms, nipples were hard under flimsy fabric, cocks were "chubby," or "fitty-cent," or maybe even "massive," if one was to judge by Mr. Jacob's bulge following his last glance at Ms. Garland. This was Louisiana and the air-conditioning was broken. You can begin any novel with that sentence and you're sure to be carried along by a swift stream of perspiration through history and psychology. No writers can do better than to live here and begin thus: *This was Louisiana and the air-conditioning was broken.* Watch humanity at its sensual worst and best, squirming to cool off, fighting for no discernible reason, drinking liquid flesh, selling their bodies for beds of ice. Cool sheets. And Trudy Helmick was from the North. Not admitting that the wires holding her flesh under the blue dress were burning and branding her skin was heroic. Trudy was a hero.

"I'll give you Miroslav Holub, a man with a rational, cool head, a scientist who writes brief glacial and funny poems. He is a Czech poet, born in Plzeň in Bohemia, which is a part of the Czech Republic where Pilsner beer and the word 'bohemian' come from. It's amazing that such a cool head could emerge from there, but only if you overlook the mechanical ingenuity of the Czechs, which rivals that of the Germans. There are no 'bohemians' in Bohemia, that comes out of romantic claptrap, and the beer is actually a kind of food!" I was practically indignant. I don't know why.

There are two regions of the world that get a bum rap on account of their names being misused by romantics: Bohemia and Transylvania. I won't go into Transylvania now. Interested readers can enter the corpus of my oeuvre and suck there the juices of Transylvania. Or take a trip there on their own, but hurry before the place merges with its image! In the case of Bohemia, there are prized crafts, especially glass, and complex puppets, and fabulous clockworks that are still being produced, as well as Pilsner beer regulated by the EU, another layer over the post-hip invasion lying atop the Velvet Revolution that overlies Charter 77 and Vaclav Havel that tops the kitsch Eighties that lie over the Soviet-tank-controlled Seventies and over postwar communist takeover, over Nazi occupation, over Czech surrealism and Švankmajer, over Kafka and Milena, over the Austrian empire, over the Enlightenment and Czech nationalism, over the ashes of Jan Hus on top of Casanova and Mozart, over Emperor Rudolf the Mad who fed his alchemists to the bears in the castle moat, and over Libuše the amazon warrior and patron saint of Prague, each layer with its own languages, German, Czech, and, after the Velvet Revolution, a bounty of English, American English, British English, Irish English, spoken by young people with beautiful bodies and intelligent faces escaping from history, their own and that of their countries, as well as from boredom, ennui, the people they knew, and their parents (who often paid for their escape). The expats opened cafes, published newsletters and magazines, held poetry readings, made art on walls and on bodies, and drank a lot, two huge-ass Pilsners for fifty cents American, and there was real absinthe to be had, prepared in teaspoons over a flaming sugar cube. Absinthe's secret poetic ingredient, wormwood, was so poisonous it had been outlawed everywhere in Europe, just like poetry, which had been outlawed by commerce; and the rebel youth in love with the ineffable, flocked to Prague to be consumed by genius, hopefully their own, but if not, by the genius of another expat, a mysterious fulgurating creature with wings and breasts and very little flesh. I saw such geniuses everywhere, haughty and starved, worshipped like gods and dreaded like shamans, gathered in conspiratorial clumps under the saints of St. Charles Bridge, throwing their empty wine boxes into the Vltava. Some of them had guitars and sang "House of the Rising Sun" in Russian, Dutch, and English. Laura stayed up all night one summer night with such a cosmopolitan outlaw gang, teaching them the proper words, "There is a house in New Orleans . . . the ruin of many a young man . . . ," etc., etc., until she staggered ecstatically home in the instant dawn (dark in summer Prague lasting maybe two hours). I saw her from the window of our fifth-floor apartment, a black-clad figure of bohemian incandescence reflected in the exploding sunlight off the cupolas of churches and monuments, her arms swinging at her side, still singing. She saw me at the window when she looked up and she squatted in greeting and peed heartily on the medieval cobblestones of the empty square where people had been hanged, revolutions unfolded, and national holidays celebrated. Her joyous stream rolled over the old stones, visible even from the fifth floor, and I'd have liked to greet her back by pissing out the window into the dawn, but I had a hard-on and couldn't get out a drop. She continued to sing and dance or prance after she came up, and did this for three or four days until she calmed down enough to sleep. She was still high when she woke up after three days, and there was nothing my dark and wise East European irony could do to convince her that the euphoria she was experiencing was the temporary after-effect of all revolutions, and that as soon as the currency stabilized and the artists ran out of money, the cloud of greyness that covers the world would slide back over everything. But why spoil her joy? Anyone who's had the good fortune to be poor and free after a revolution knows the feeling: it's like standing naked in a warm downpour while ejaculating. Can't beat that. Coming alone or with one or a few others can approximate the feeling, but nothing beats it.

Next summer (Laura wasn't there) a virgin tried to give herself to me for poetry. She looked like Letitia "Red" Klein, next in line for a ghost.

"Miss Klein, I cannot contain my joy at your fleeting resemblance to someone I once knew!"

Letitia Klein's hair was fiery red, hence her nickname, "Red." In fact, now that I let my eyes roam over the heads of my poetry students, all their hair ran the gamut of red, from shades of golden-red to glowing embers. I am a lucky teacher. To have inherited, in my last semester of spreading the impossible affliction of poetry, a room full of red! I thank you, Poe! The virgin whom Letitia resembled was a quiet, slight girl who vibrated on the steps of the University of Prague building in which was lodged the American poetry school where I made some extra cash teaching summers. She sat on the steps buzzed on youth and caffeine and listened to me say things she didn't hear, so when I asked her up to my room she followed me. My room, once again on the fifth floor, was powerfully buffeted by wind. All over the building the wind slammed windows shut, sounding like gunfire. I'd left my window open and it banged when I opened the door, a thunderclap. The fury startled me and I shut it quickly. When I turned back to ask the girl to come in, I saw that she had shed her jeans and tee shirt and was sitting in her panties on the sofa bed. She had goosebumps all over and no breasts to speak of. I hadn't considered (not very much anyway) the possibility of seducing her. I'd asked her up, but I'd been almost certain that she'd resist the feeble entreaties I'd already (subconsciously) decided would be feeble. I didn't expect a naked, wispy, shaking girl body looking about thirteen years old (though she was eighteen, she swore) to be sitting on my sofa like an Aztec sacrifice. I put a paternal arm around her bony shoulder, and I told her to put her clothes back on, but she rolled away and pulled off the last bit of cloth. Without panties, there seemed to be even less of her, the small fleece of red down over the thin squiggly line between her legs subtracting rather than adding to her mass. What are you doing? I asked her silently. I'm a virgin, it stands between me and the world, can you take care of it? she answered in like manner. I looked at her lit up like Joan of Arc ready for martyrdom as an insane happiness beamed from her eyes. I asked her if she felt beautiful and she said "yes," and I had no doubt about it. She put her arms behind her head and let me look at her very naked nude body, the nakedest she could possibly make it, and all around us was medieval Prague, Wenceslaus Square and all that history, and it's probably that history more than anything else that made me insist urgently that she descend from the pyre, put her armor back on, panties with tiny blue flowers, bluejeans and the tee shirt with a gold-sequined fleur-de-lys on it. When she did, I saw some workers on scaffolding in a building across the street looking into my curtainless window, and I laughed. It's a wonder they hadn't fallen off their scaffold. They were young Czechs, born into the benighted dawn of capitalism, restoring old Prague after decades of commie neglect. I saw Milan Kundera's window-washer in grey old Prague looking at his sad girlfriend waiting to have sex in the monochromatic Stalinist building now being returned to imperial glory.

I walked the girl to the creaky elevator, still dank and unrestored, and I was sad because another layer of history had settled somehow between the summer before and this one. And now it's been a decade since the elevator with the virgin went down, and I'm sure that the young poet is no longer a virgin, I believe that she is a professor. She is a professor at Charles University in a Disneyfied, pricey, pastel-colored, touristy Prague void of intellectual window-washers, bohemians, or post-commie Rimbauds.

"Who do I remind you of?" Letitia Klein said flirtily.

"Joan of Arc."

"Oh." Disappointed. Really. This was Catholic Louisiana, Miss Klein was from New Orleans, and being reminded of Joan of Arc was in no way exceptional. There was even a statue of Joan of Arc at Decatur Street before the French Market. The locals call her "Joanie on the Pony." To be reminded of Joan of Arc in New Orleans is like being reminded of windmills in Holland.

"I have no intention of hearing voices. We'll leave that to my Aunt Clara, the nun." Letitia Klein said judiciously.

"I'm sorry. I meant that you remind me of someone I knew once, who reminded me of Joan of Arc. I'm expressing myself very clumsily for a teacher of English. Your Aunt Clara is a nun?" I'd thought she was Jewish but no, I saw now, German Catholic. Louisiana had deep German roots, going back to several waves of immigration during the nineteenth century.

"I come from a big family in German Settlement. Everybody I knew in grade school had an aunt who was a nun. My mother says that all the nuns are old now and that if nobody my age follows in the tradition, nuns are going to die out. Aunt Clara was a teacher." She looked genuinely sad.

I wondered if the nuns who'd been chased by the latest hurricane from their convent on St. Charles Avenue had come back. "Your Aunt Clara . . . was she at the St. Charles convent?"

"No, she was at a house in Tangipahoa."

"Isn't that where they put the mad nuns?" Bennigan said, tactful as usual.

"She's just old. It's a house for very old nuns."

There are a number of homes for old or disturbed monastics in Catholic southern Louisiana and New Orleans. The city was settled by Sieur de Bienville in an inhospitable swamp surrounded by a huge lake and the Mississippi River, dedicated to his Sun King, Louis XIV, and patronized by the maid of Orleans, burned at the stake when still in her teens, but no matter how deranged the history, one thing was for sure: the Inquisition was never allowed to set foot in the New World. When the Church sent an inquisitor to New Orleans, he was sent packing back to Spain. He returned chastised years later and dedicated himself to ministering to Native Americans and doing good works. If nuns and monks went mad after lifetimes of kind work in the subtropics, it was no sin.

"Miss Letitia," I said, "I have here the perfect Catholic for you, the poet Jack Kerouac, but just in case, here are some other choices . . . Kaufman, Bob and Shirley, Kafka, Kerouac, Kama Sutra, Kazantzakis . . ." I was reaching way over the ledge here, and Miss Klein, who was no rube, caught me sneaking in the Kama Sutra.

"The Kama Sutra, that's the Indian sex manual! Can I really take that for my Ghost-Companion?"

They broke up. Bennigan shouted, "I'll test it!" Even the sober Mr. Borden smiled. Chloe put her head on her desk and pretended to weep. Jack Ferris winked. And Letitia Klein blushed, looking more like the Virgin of Prague than I even remembered.

I am a very bad man. "I don't know how the Kama Sutra got in there. It's poetry. But it's still the kind that'll get me fired if I assign it to you and you tell your mom and your mom tells the school and the school tells the police and the police tells the judge! Horrors!" I looked at her face for pity. There was none. Only merriment. Kids. But Borden hummed the Ink Spots song about the blabbering trees telling all to the breeze.

The breeze absorbed what the trees blabbered and carried it off in a puffy gossip-cloud. So this was cloud-computing! I was struck by the novelty of it: nothing we said here in class would ever be lost! Cloud-computing, which was this dense fog that absorbed every communication on the planet, was busy carrying off poetry and its assignments to large black cubes similar to the meteorite at Mecca, where they passed through grids that separated the seditious from the inefficient and perhaps the poetic from the unpoetic. These vast petabytes of stored communication awaited the study of superbeings who would devise uses from them. This was what my students had been designed for: they were superbeings that, far from being helpless and silly as their tastes in music and clothes might have appeared to an old fuddy-duddy like myself, were in fact superabsorbent and modular, techno-sponges for all that could be sensed or said.

I recognized this optimistic sentiment with resigned weariness. It occurred punctually like Death holding her scythe in the astronomical clock in the tower of Prague's Town Hall. The predominantly red mass of my students' hair bounced in a single wave toward me. I raised my hand to my

face. Their hair was going to punish me for my timid pedagogy. They had signed up for poetry class, and I was just
dishing out vanilla assignments, required reading for twenti-
eth-century bookworms. Humanities departments in our
universities, the menacing hair flaring about me proclaimed,
infantilize everyone, students and teachers alike, because
there are no adults in the system, and by "adults" we mean
people who understand the cloud-computing of all information, including language.

"We have no time!" I pleaded with the swirling hair-
cloud. "We've been in a crisis of time! Minutes ago your
teachers were students themselves, then student-teachers,
then assistant professors, then tenured professors, and the
whole process was uninterrupted by anything more than a
summer vacation in Europe. We are teaching in an institution run by institutionalized people who have invested all
their time into the institution! The lunatics run the asylum!
We all have an investment in keeping the racket going! It's all
a pyramid scheme, people, like everything else in the world
now, from economies to banking, and you are at the bottom
of the pyramid!"

Ouch! The collective hair braided itself into several whips,
a cat-o-nine-tails actually, and began to lash me. "Stop it!" I
begged it. "I'm ready to admit it, Miss Letitia! Your Aunt
Clara was the last honest teacher in America! She believed in
the Akashic records where all that is said and done is not
only stored, sifted, and analyzed, but also judged and pun-
ished. She went mad in a world bent on remaining infantile.
Not in the way Jesus meant it when he said that we should
be like children, but in some idiotic way, like a Rube Gold-
berg machine of busyness. Whatever there still is in us that
would like to take the world seriously is stifled in these

schools of yours. I freely admit it! The computing cloud has just taken off with my admission, to be stored with all the others. We will fall down, eventually, and it will be only minutes from now!"

Their hair stopped lashing me and drew back to the tops of their heads. As their faces came back into focus, I laughed, relieved that the computing cloud hadn't made off with all of them. They looked so endearing, so *particular*.

"Your Aunt Clara, what do you remember her saying? I mean, do you remember anything that she liked to say?"

"Oh, sure," Letitia laughed, not a trace of martyrdom about her. "She used to say that a nickel sure isn't a nickel anymore. And she said that people weren't people anymore, and 'Thank God, I'm a nun,' she said, 'because I don't have to buy new shoes every time I go out.' Oh, and she said once that people who didn't pray were just big intestines with food going in and out and no respect for anything."

I was with the old nun on all those things, and so was dear Letitia Klein, who did not deserve in any way to be saddled with one of America's most famous drunk writers, a man who rejected his daughter Jan Kerouac, a wonderful writer herself who died young emulating daddy's bad habits.

"All the old people complain about the prices of things," Borden said. "They don't realize how much it takes to make something. Like milk."

Their faces began merging, combining to make the famous *Time* magazine cover of the twenty-first-century human, a face with a profusion of features in it. Well, of course, we had already run out of Chinese and Indonesians and every other source of cheap labor. We were now in search of the inner Chinese or Indonesian, that laborer who could somehow make enough stuff for our double to consume. When old people complain about the prices of things because a nickel was worth something in their day, it is because they knew what kind of work you had to do for a nickel. People who now pay a hundred dollars for a gallon of gas or ten thousand for a hotel room won't hear that sort of thing if they can somehow get hold of thousands of dollars; it simply doesn't matter to them how high the prices get if the work is easy; and it's easy because somebody else does it. It's even OK when half the cash vanishes into the pockets of middlemen. There is no point in recapitulating Marx, children, but your merged face looks worried about the future when one of your personalities will have to work for a living. *Well, that's not what I'm here for!* I shouted at the face, intimidated no longer by its pleading look that, unlike their merged hair, did not threaten me with the consequences of my rants.

There is always a moment in poetry class when the mysterious musk of ill-defined desire turns into economic argument. It may be hunger; we were all hungry, having gone without food for centuries, or at least since class started. Once again, it was the sober Mr. Borden who clarified the matter. I would have rather heard from the quiet Mr. Rios or Ms. Washington, who were perhaps in closer temporal proximity to the wretched of the earth of whom it seems that we were speaking, but neither Ms. Washington nor Mr. Rios appeared to evince any interest in the question, though they looked alert enough.

"The reason there are no riots on the streets," said the heir to the empire of milk, "is because all of it happens *gradually*. The only thing that hasn't been gradually inflating is the rate of the gradual. What used to be gradual is a lot steeper now, so steep that a user of the word 'gradually' in

1920, like my grandmother, would gasp to hear what it might refer to today."

I saw her, the flapper poet, rotating in wonder inside Diana.

"How many pairs of shoes would you say your grandmother had?" asked Chloe, recalling that in the Roaring Twenties, like in our Gilded Nineties, value was measured in stylish wear, not vulgar coin. The gold standard of that value then, like now, was shoes. She herself was wearing some sort of satin slippers with magic-marker doodles on them.

I liked her question. My friend Mary, the heiress, as it happens, to another milk fortune (what is it about milk?), went about barefoot most of the time, but when time came to dress up she threw open the doors of a vast chamber filled to the rafters with myriad shoes, a closet peerless in my mind until Imelda Marcos's was revealed.

"Thousands," grinned Matthew Borden. "My father carted a full truck of shoes to the Goodwill. A pity, really. They'd bring a fortune on eBay."

A pity indeed, but then I recalled that Mary's collection came mostly from Goodwill, and I was certain that the shoes of the Silo Goddess had another useful and entertaining life before finally ending on eBay. Maybe what I was doing here was assigning more than G-Cs. Maybe I was recycling the old poets themselves, giving them new young bodies to live in, reincarnating them.

A pleasant hum followed this brief immersion into the subject of shoes, settling the economic argument. One can have the nightmare or the dream. The nightmare is an American Jabba the Hutt sitting atop a mountain of shoes made by barefoot slaves skinning animal corpses for the leather. The dream is that, after all that work, everyone gets to go out wearing fashionable footwear. The most valuable commodity, right after human energy, is *style*. If styles don't change to arouse us to trade in yesterday's model for today's, the world collapses. Style feeds capital, and so it can never be allowed to devolve into the familiar, it must aspire to multidimensionality, to complexity . . . to poetry.

The Cloud descended again, absorbing everything in class, and distributed it to the global grids.

"I'll take Kerouac," said Letitia Klein.

"OK," I said, "but it's got to be the young Kerouac, the one Edie Parker fell in love with in 1940 when she and Jack were both eighteen. The one Allen Ginsberg and Cassady fell in love with. Not the drunk, foul-mouthed later Kerouac of Lowell, Mass, who didn't talk to his old friends and rejected Jan. Yes, you can have Kerouac, Miss Klein, but when you're done with the intoxicated giddiness of his youth, give him up. Hand him over to Aunt Clara to straighten out. Your Aunt Clara belonged to the age of frugality, Letitia, attractive to us because we are profligate. She skipped the whole age of consumption, and she may be crazy but she's better off."

Letitia looked offended. I shouldn't have called Aunt Clara crazy right after handing her old Jack.

I wish that life was kinder to us poets, all filled in our youth with gladness, like Wordsworth said, only to become monsters to our children. I can tell you about lots of famous daddies' children who wanted to step into their writerly shoes, like my friend Aram Saroyan, the son of William Saroyan. His Armenian daddy divorced his Jewish mommy when he found out that she was Jewish. Aram is the son of survivors of two of the twentieth century's worst genocides. He is the son of intolerance, split in two by his mutually repelling survivor parents. And yes, Aram is a very good writer and survives in spite of it all. And then there are Jan Kerouac and Bill Burroughs, Jr., who did not.

"Kerouac in his youth," I said, "was a Buddhist of sorts, a hipster jazz Zen Buddhist who riffed in poetry published as 'Mexico City Blues.' You can read those and maybe they'll inspire you to riff. They are loose, funny, stoned poems."

Yes, and stop right there. Don't go on the road. Stay home. Raise a family. In the end, Kerouac himself drank his way to that revelation, and hoped that posterity would leave him alone. No such luck, Jack. We poets hunger for the inexplicable, which is instinctual and feeds on imagination and cannot live without stories. To write poetry you need Imagination, but if you use it too much, life and her stories will rob you of it. The only good imagination is unused imagination. Aunt Clara doesn't need shoes. She has no use for your fancy, either. With the proviso, of course, that being mad, she might be unable to control it. When she taught school, you can be sure you didn't pass her class without memorizing the Ten Commandments.

I terminated these reactionary thoughts and said, "Here is an example of Zen poetry, it's a koan, I wrote it just now: 'What's better at telling time? Your watch or your wallet?'"

Several people raised their hands.

"Mr. Borden."

"Wallet."

"Maybe," I said. "I just made that up so I don't know the answer yet. Might as well take yours. Money means you've put in time, but they are not equivalent like the saw has it. Still, you may be right."

"I'm right," mumbled Borden, deep in consideration of his own problems with money, namely having too much of it.

The last half hour of class is the Hour of Compassion, which, like the Hour of Death, can be thirty minutes or a week. In the Hour of Compassion, pity for the young enters

96

my heart. All weariness and cynicism wash from me like sand under a shower. I await this variety of exhaustion with some apprehension. I get to feel the human form of all my victims and I become as dim as a novelist. My wax wings melt and I become the plaything of affections. Some of this Compassion is for the past, but most of it is fortune-telling, which is to say useless. Borden was a bottle-fed baby crying for his mother's milk and will be a kindly paterfamilias who'll make sure that his own children won't suffer the same fate. Chloe will pierce herself in the same places the bullets will enter Hillary's soldier body a month from now. Jason Jacob and Beatrice Garland will hold hands and jump off a Mississippi River tour boat, leaving behind a collaboratively composed epitaph. Jack Ferris will bankrupt the prestigious brokerage firm he works for when he invests billions in a Ferlinghetti poem–inspired scheme, and lose it all. "Red" Klein will work briefly as a stripper at Big Daddy's on Bourbon Street, then go to stewardess school and marry a rich cocaine dealer she'll die with when their yacht blows up. Or she'll become the last nun in New Orleans, right after being fired from Big Daddy's for refusing to freelance. I know. This is melodrama, not compassion, oracular or otherwise. But how can anyone become anything other than what the culture prescribes for them? Or what the tired teacher envisions at his Hour of Compassion?

"Can we take a break and go to the bathroom?" Chloe asked, on behalf of millions and millions of poets.

"Again? Again?" If I was exasperated, it wasn't because I was a monster, but this need to constantly piss really cut into my compassion. "Go ahead," I said, "but be back in a New York minute!"

This time I decided to take a restroom break myself. I went to the professors' Men's Room on the second floor, a place of majestic faience and private stalls where, I imagined, my colleagues held their puds with dignity and let go a flood of professional resentments. There was something solemn and sorrowful about this bathroom forbidden to students. Apartheid still reigned here, keeping the effluvia of professors separate from the discharges of pupils. I pissed smugly on academia, which is a way of saying that I pissed on myself, which I do, regularly, to extinguish my pretensions. While I was peeing I didn't think I was immortal, but felt something very much like it. It hurts me, it really does, to know so much and to have to invent everything. I could just be a damn professor like all the dinosaurs that spray these stalls, but I can't. I'd have to give up being a poet, not that anyone knows what the hell that is, but that's exactly the point. The professors are not afflicted by the identity crisis that is my only subject. They go about in the certainty of their well-cultivated fields and keep adding what they can to the antheap of text before them. My job, I think, is to burn all that came before me—by handing my predecessors to the students to misunderstand, if it comes to that, which it obviously does. There are sixteen million people writing poetry in the United States, and each one has a passing acquaintance with the art. We could be a useful voting bloc if we hadn't dedicated ourselves solely to the pursuit of the Inexplicable. In other words, if we voted like we lived, not like we wrote. All those who call ourselves "poets" could constitute a movement dedicated to ... what? Fracturing the complete sentence? Sketching delicate sentiments in Japanese ink on the public mind? Complicating the human psyche so that it might grow new extremities to merge with both animals and microprocessors? Millions of poets out there, splitting hairs, overrefining the world's languages as if they were crude oil, and here I am, pissing in the faculty room instead of opening a trench into the civic brain and pissing into that! NAB (the New American Brain) and the masses of the unemployed listened in wonder to my raving as I zipped up.

When I returned to the classroom the students were all staring at me. I looked down at my zipper. It was in order. I hadn't peed my pants, either.

"What?" I stared back.

They kept staring.

Then it hit me. Time had stopped. I was an anachronism. Time stopped like a stream of piss in midflow, freezing like a bronze waterfall. And then I understood why the technology in fairly recent (early twenty-first century, let's say) movies looks dated, while old movies (from, let's say, the mid-twentieth century) look stylish. It was the fact that in the old movies every object was a perfect anachronism. Everything about the people of the 1920s or 1930s was how it should be, how it would always be. A true anachronism never changes, it is immortal—once it attains venerable anachronistic status. And that's not easy. The recent movies will become anachronistic in time, but that is only when the present is truly done with them. Until then, they will be merely awkward, like kids kept back a grade, or an inexpert plumber fiddling with the wrong fittings. I stared back at the future and it kept staring at me with eyes of wonder. I had made it past awkwardness to the anachronistic stage. I was a fossil. Henceforth, I would keep my form for all who'd stare at me. There was nothing, short of lingering DNA, that could change my status. I was *there*. A fossil is immortal because it has moved out of Fast Human Time (FHT) into Instructive Slow Time (IST). I looked back from inside the frame of rock where I'd been trapped by the Late Ice Age (LIA) and I asked the class:

"What are the uses of Immortality? Or let me put it another way: if you were Elvis or JFK or Marilyn Monroe, you would be immortal, right? I mean, you would be so immortal that no book ever written on you, no new revelation, could ever change your iconic status! Let's say somebody found out that JFK was bisexual? Would it change anything about those initials, JFK?"

Betty Garland raised her hand. "J. Edgar Hoover was gay."

"Yes, but the subject is immortality, not proclivity. I only used 'bisexual' as a possible revision of JFK. True immortality is several degrees past fame. Britney Spears was famous, or maybe notorious, but she was not immortal. Madonna hovered between fame and immortality, not least because she borrowed the name of another immortal. How many of you would like to be famous?"

Chloe, Bennigan, and Jack Ferris raised their hands.

"How many of you would like to be immortal like John Keats or JFK?"

Nobody.

"Mr. Ferris, why would you want to be famous but not immortal?"

"Well, like Borden said, it's a matter of degrees. Can't be immortal before you're famous, so I'll be gradual."

"Me, too," said Bennigan, "I'd like to be carved into Mount Rushmore but I'd have to do something to deserve it first . . ."

"Let's look at it another way," I said. "Let's say you're a paleontologist and one day you find a fossil that's a big clue to your discipline. That fossil is immortal, right? Now, was that fossil ever famous? Maybe, but I doubt it. We are talking three million years old, before TV. The only reason that fossil is immortal is because it survived! The rock it's trapped inside of survived geological cataclysms and human history. The fossil is immortal not just because the professor found it but because there is no way to look at it except through the immensity of time. That fossil cannot be anything but what it is, no matter what anybody might say or think about it."

Trudy Helmick followed the argument with interest. "Sure, but what if it's a fake? Our church believes that the world is six thousand years old and that the devil planted a lot of fake evidence. I'm not saying that I really think that, but I don't know." She closed her eyes and said, "Ugh! I can't believe I just said that!"

"You might have a point, Miss Helmick!" I did not dismiss the idea of the devil as a skillful forger who had faked what we call reality. Still, whether fake or not, immortality operated in every conceivable reality, including that of Trudy's church, for the simple reason that Time is an uncontested dimension. When I'd asked what the uses of immortality are, I wanted to know the answer. And now it occurred to me, as I looked at Trudy's sturdy mortal frame, that immortality confers freedom. Unlike fame, immortality doesn't need a press agent. Iconic presence is beyond opinion, therefore I was immune to ridicule. That was a ridiculous notion, as Borden pointed out:

"Everybody's immortal if they believe they have a soul. It's a hell of a lot harder to be famous. Or rich," he added significantly.

That sort of threw me. Class warfare was back.

Well, maybe. The past smelled like cigarettes, urine, and sperm. No more speculation. I put my foot down—on the accelerator. No more staring. I still had poets to give away. The evil Santa wasn't yet done with his distribution. The bell of the Hour of Compassion had stopped ringing.

"Sylvia Minneaux!" I called. A tall girl rose from a tiny desk. Sylvia was athletic and brisk, wearing jodhpurs, an elephant under her, hair razored to her scalp by a nineteenth-century Punjabi barber. Maybe not, but she was certainly statuesque, with dark eyebrows that met over two spinning angry brown orbs. I rubbed my eyes. I found it hard to believe that I hadn't noticed her. It wasn't possible: poetry students are rarely this stately and so from another time. They tend to runtiness, lack of sleep and protein, sallow complexions, skin explosions, leaking libidos. Here was a picture of health with a French name, standing before me, ready for her Ghost-Companion, a Minotaur perhaps, or a Monster, something that starts with M but big enough to contain Mars. And she was angry because she was hungry.

"Henry Michaux!" I thundered. "Henry Michaux took Mescaline and wrote Miserable Miracle, all great M accomplishments, and his name, like yours, had blessèd if not downright vertiginous waters at the end! He was also a Maverick of French poetry, a Male!"

"I'll take him," Miss Mineaux said curtly, and sat down at the tiny desk that reverberated long after her body was settled on the wood. The class was impressed. So was I. About Michaux I knew little. He wrote lovely poems and radio plays, traveled a lot throughout the Americas, took psychedelics early, like Aldous Huxley, but of his *substance* I knew little. I was certain that this state of ignorance would soon cease, however, because Sylvia Minneaux was going to put an abrupt end to my ignorance. A horsewoman was coming to the mountain. Muhammad stood very still.

I allowed time to pass. There was only a bit of it left in the world. Every day there would be less of it, until a year from now, two at most, all these young people would look up startled from their multitasking and say simultaneously, "Remember that silence in poetry class? We used to have time back then."

I had few thoughts now, but I was lightly embarrassed by my preferences in poetry, forged by mid-Sixties Grove Press anthologies and City Lights collections, and the opinions and work of my poet-friends who had been formed and had remained loyal to the very same poetry and its publishers. Were Barney Rosset and Lawrence Ferlinghetti the genii in the brain-bottles of millions of my victims? Lordee. If anything consoles me now it is that attached to these poets and their publishers and my friends and their work were *stories*. I had thousands of stories to tell about these people and their products because this was my life, a life spent hanging out, talking, writing poetry, alone or with others, seeing twisted shapes in the night and crisp aphorisms at dawn. My life is full of tragic and funny stories that happened to people known to me, and I was their sole keeper, at least in the narrative forms I invented for telling them! So who is there accusing me of generalizing, of using language like an umbrella? I have the details, I can empty my pockets. Away, demon, away!

At this point, a cat came through the door. It was as if Beatrice Garland's tattoo leapt from her shoulder and came into the classroom. The stunned silence was full of cats.

Every soul in the room knew a cat or many cats. Some of them had a cat at present. Miss Garland carried hers in the flesh. Cat stories, told by relatives at weddings and funerals, stuck in their minds like roots of hair. Cats traversed the lives of my students since birth. America is a pet-loving nation and cats are our national pet. Of dogs I've spoken often, but let's rest for a moment in this classroom full of mental cats and one live, black pussy with blue eyes strolling in the open door.

It is a warm spring day in Louisiana, a season that might be called summer elsewhere, but here, amid flowering magnolias and dizzily scented boughs of sweet-olive, between reddish brick buildings in the "Georgian style," a cat strolls into the classroom where "Introduction to Writing Poetry" meets for the first time.

There are famous cats, like Bulgakov's Russian-speaking puss in "The Master and Margarita," and Julio Cortázar's cat that returned to the Pont Neuf in Paris twice a week for several years after he died, but this was not a famous cat. Not yet. Twelve pairs of eyes turned to this cat, astonished by the feline, but the cat was unfazed. It strode in and it leapt onto my desk. There, it stretched, looked at me, put its head on its paws, and sprawled for all the world like a late student. I involuntarily stroked its head. One of its ears twitched. That's all.

The cat was warm and alive under my fingers. I had two thoughts: the year before, my poet-friend Denisa Comă-nescu, who is an editor at a publishing house, asked me to write a novel with a cat in it. The logo of her imprint features a leaping cat. I laughed, but Denisa was serious. "You write me a book with a cat in it, and you'll be rich," she predicted, looking rather Egyptian. And the second thought wasn't a thought, but an e-mail I'd received that very morning from

another poet, Ruxandra Cesereanu, in response to my bland
assertion that I felt the need to write a book about poets and
animals:

*Ti-am spus vreodata despre motanul Tony sau Toni al
parintilor mei? S-a nascut fara coada (are doar un ciuf
de iepure), din motive de incest, nascut fiind el din o
sora si un frate. Seamana cu pisicile de angora, dar are
si ceva birmanez, are un cap minunat, parsivul, o fru-
musete. Dar e homosexual, are tendinta sa isi sodom-
izeze fiii! Daca nu-i mingiiat, face urit. Pe tatal meu s-a
obisnuit sa il pupe cu botul pe chelie! Si se pare ca e si
un pisic muzical. Si-acu te las, amigo mio mustachudo!
pupacindu-te, Ru.*

Did I ever tell you about my parents' tomcat Toni or
Tony? He was born without a tail (has only a tuft like
a rabbit) because of incest, the result of being born to a
sister and brother. He looks a bit like an angora, but
has something burmese about him, a marvelous head,
a lazy beauty. He is also homosexual and has a tendency to sodomize his descendants. He likes to lick my
father's bald head. I have to go now, my mustachioed
friend! Ru.

I call Ruxandra Ru and she insists that I have a mustache
(like a cat) although I haven't had one since I shaved it off in
Venice near the end of the last century. Ruxandra is a cat
herself, in that esthetic and willful manner that some women
adopt because they admire felines above all creatures, certainly above men and dogs. Laura has always had a cat, and
she becomes very unhappy when her cat dies. She must have
another right away, a purring engine that sits at her feet

while she reads history. Her oldest cat, Tipitina, Tippy for short, died recently at age twenty-one. Women, especially women poets, like to praise the independence and beauty of cats, and at some point in their feminine-artistic development they study the history of cats, and pen poems in the Metropolitan Museum or other museums, standing before a mummified cat buried alongside a royal. At some point in their life-journey all women learn that cats used to be worshipped as gods in one or another ancient culture, but they will refuse to hear, if someone has the bad taste of voicing it, that the cooking of cats is widespread in China and elsewhere, and that the majority of the ancients ate rather than worshipped cats. Fie, spit in your eye!

A majestic presence stretched on the desk before me. I felt as if I had acquired new authority, something pharaonic perhaps, as if the act of this feline had been a sign of election for the entire Introduction to Writing Poetry class, not just a freaky incident due to an open classroom door and the well-known existence of feral cats on campus. Lonely coeds fed the wild cats by the campus lakes, and word had spread. Our Southern university was as full of cats as ancient Rome. I stroked the indifferent pussy once more and called out the name of the next student. We were quickly running out of time.

"Carlos Rios!"

A shy, bespectacled (not from EyeMasters), scrawny kid looked at me, scared. Was he scared of me or of the cat? Carlos looked Indio, Mexican, and American. Hispanic, in short, but with something old about him, maybe the Spanish language glistening on his upper lip. Carlos was going to be adopted by the females in this class like a stray cat, I thought.

"I read the paper, and today there was an article about this town in Ohio that's offering five dollars for every stray cat," said Carlos eying the tabby ruefully. "Maybe it escaped from Ohio!"

"That would be a thousand miles it traveled," deadpanned Bennigan.

"We should name it, it's the class cat now," said Chloe.

I suggested we name her (was it a her?) "Intro to Writing Poetry."

Several students called out, "Here . . . here . . . Intro . . . pss . . . psss."

Intro lifted his (was it a him?) head and looked at the class as if they were a boring herd of gnus. Too big to eat, too small to worry about. That was the weary look of ages since Egypt. Intro knew people. These poetry students didn't look like the feral-cat hunters of Ohio. They had kinder eyes. Intro had the look of a cat who'd adopted many kinds of businesses in the past. She (he?) was the kind of cat that walks into a bar, leaps onto the counter, and lounges there for the drunks to pet it. Intro was a touch of home for people who didn't have one. Solace for drunks. Object of study for poets.

"We should name it after a poet," observed Hillary Adams.

Hillary was familiar with the campus cats. She knew that her lab had adopted a cat and named it Mendeleyev, though people called her Mandy. Her French class had one named Proust. And in her other required English class, "Survey of British Literature," there lived Byron, a giant black tomcat.

"Schroedinger's," suggested Borden.

Really. Somebody had overeducated the poor fellow.

"Sappho," said Chloe.

That was good. "Sappho . . . pss . . . psss . . ." went the class, and the kitty again regarded the crowd, more attentively this time. It preferred Sappho to Intro. So be it. Another Sappho was born. She lay her head back on her paws and there was the faint sound of a lyre drifting in from afar as Sappho purred.

I turned to pedagogy: "Self-consciousness is a beautiful thing if the self is conscious of its beauty. Need a self so beautiful also be self-conscious? In this matter, cats have it all over us. Not only do they not concern themselves with esthetics, they don't even question the miracle of knowing how to pose. Something in their slick bodies knows that they are being watched and that they must look their best. That *something* is a poetic knowledge we will learn in this class."

The young bodies at their school desks straightened, flexed, stretched. The hunger in them drove their animal selves to the fore. And this is how poetry is taught, I replied with some satisfaction to all those people who, over the years, questioned the possibility of teaching poetry. In their minds few things were unteachable, but poetry was one of those. I wish they'd been right. Unfortunately, poetry was exceedingly teachable. One reached for the end of any thread in the tangled ball of yarn of what we know and pulled: the thing unraveled and that was poetry. I had trained thousands to pull a thread from this ball of life-yarn, and now they trail strings wherever they walk, true kittens of capitalism. An eighteenth-century poet locked up overnight in a modern poetry library would not experience the same shock he would if faced with a car or a computer: the words are in English, the sentence structure looks familiar, even the blank verse is understandable. The content might be hard going at times, especially if there are cars and computers in it, but he would have no trouble identifying the grand themes of love and terror, and he would quickly figure out the relatively new expressions of awkwardness and embarrassment. Humor would be new to him only to the extent that it might lack ruddiness or vigor, as if the hale laughter of his day had been blanched like an almond. He would sniff at modern irony: "translation for the ladies!" He might experience some disorientation before the modern insistence on fruits and vegetables, animals and brand names, but he would attribute it to a taxonomic disease, a virus of the concrete. Such ills were not unknown in his day, they defined the *prose* of naturalists and adventurers. One expected Humboldt or Darwin to name and describe everything because that was their job, to come upon new things to name and describe. Theirs was the first gaze. The poets' job was to cast a weary second glance on the world and to look fondly into eternal sentiments with a musical insistence that made them new. Love, for instance. An eighteenth-century poet did not *bring* love to the object of his attention, he *elicited* it and then and only then did he pronounce Oh! Love was in all things, a fundamental substance activated by the poet's gaze. Everything else was stories to illustrate this eternal truth, including ruddy vulgar stories that made the listeners howl with glee. Modern poetry, it would seem to him, had stripped, or rather scooped out, eternity from the core of things, and had flattened them to see and classify and name drily, after which operation (some) poetry proceeded to re-romanticize the whole thing by means of interjections and projections, like archeologists reassembling smashed pots. Why, oh why, would lament the eighteenth-century poet, must you do this? Happily, by then it would be morning and the library reopened, allowing him to slip unobserved back to his own time.

"Carlos Rios, how would you like to have Rimbaud?" I was becoming generous because I was reaching the end of the alphabet. Normally, I award Rimbaud at midterm to my best student, but I was feeling magnanimous as I watched the eighteenth-century poet scurry out of the library and vanish into the bright light. I could advance to the nineteenth century and hand out my treasure, Arthur Rimbaud, who quit writing when he was the same age as Carlos Rios.

"Is this like the Big Brother thing?" Carlos was suspicious.

"Yes, but he's dead and quit writing poetry when he was no older than you, but since he'll be your Ghost-Companion you will consult with him on your assignments. You can ask questions about life of your G-C, if you want. A ghost is like a book you open to find the answer to a question. You ask and listen and the ghost goes, 'Hey, Carlos, you shouldn't have so many burgers, man. Bad for your heart.' That's how caring ghosts are. Of course, if you're feeling bad and you're having girlfriend problems, you can go, 'Hey, Rimbaud, what am I doing wrong, 'cause she just turns over in bed and won't even let me tell her a bedtime story?'"

"Maybe a bedtime story is not what she wants," said Chloe.

"Whatever," I said.

At the time this Introduction to Writing Poetry class was taking place, "whatever" had replaced "like" and "you know" as the favorite transition for the young, and I must say that I preferred it. "Whatever" felt more meaningful, like a flattening out of the unexpected depths opened by what was said. The young know that everything they say is profound, especially if it is addressed to authority, or is in any way serious. Once a serious sequence of words has welled out of a young person in the presence of authority, the only choice is to flatline it, to take out the peaks and valleys that always show up. They could say, "When I said that I wanted to battle a robot on a field of corn chips, I didn't mean it to sound so mean," or they could say, "Whatever." How much more sensible and more universal.

"Well, that's easy," said Carlos. "I'm supposed to make an A in math this semester, so I ask this Rimbaud what should I do, but if he says 'Study!,' how do I know it's Rimbaud and not anybody else, because anybody could tell me that?"

"Well, let's see." I googled "The Drunken Boat." "Look, here is what I found, in Ted Berrigan's translation, '*And I have seen what other men sometimes have thought they've seen.*' That's a pretty good answer, don't you think? It's not so much about studying, but looking at your math problems with new eyes so that you might see '*what other men sometimes have thought they've seen.*'"

Turns out Carlos Rios was pretty good at math, he was one of the University's math olympians and a chess master. He confessed all this to show his complete faith in Rimbaud.

"OK, but what about absinthe, homosexuality, and slave-trading?" said the ever-threatening Mr. Borden. "What if the Rimbaud who answers the questions is not the young genius poet, but the later drug addict and slave trader?"

"There are thousands of Rimbauds, Mr. Borden. In addition to the one you just mentioned, there are the reincarnated Rimbauds, people like young Patti Smith and Jim Morrison, all of them huddled under the umbrella of the name 'Rimbaud,' but they do not interest me or Mr. Rios. The only Rimbaud we care about is the one who responds to the bibliomancy you'll perform on his poems, isn't that right, Carlos?"

Carlos wasn't sure. He looked at Borden, he looked at me. "I'll tell you next week."

The seminar was beginning to draw to a close; we had only minutes left. I looked at Anita Washington, who had so far said nothing, looking very pretty in jeans and a tight black tee that displayed a red marijuana leaf. She looked familiar, and I remembered that I'd seen her picture in the student newspaper with an article on college women who'd auditioned for the yearly *Playboy* issue on colleges. She had been the only one to give her real name and allow herself to be photographed. She'd been pretty candid, I was struck by it, she'd described the session, the poses they made her strike, the bright lights, all in a matter-of-fact way, no frills, that's just what you do if you want America to see your body.

"Miss Washington, I give you Walt Whitman!" My generosity at this point was exceeded only by my impatience. I hadn't planned to give dead poets this much work. They are busy people in the afterlife, having to look after their editions and fans.

Anita smiled a pretty smile. "We had him in high school, *Leaves of Grass*, right?"

Everyone used the excuse to study her breasts, having no doubt recognized her as well. In the laughter that followed, I could hear Whitman clearly. "*And your very flesh shall be a great poem.*" About that, I had no doubt.

"I wrote a poem on Whitman . . . it's right here, somewhere." Miss Washington searched her laptop. "Here it is. It's called 'Walt Whitman, Poet Who Believed in Equality': *Walt Whitman sang of Lincoln. My grampa said, 'Lincoln is a Cadillac,' but no, he's the reason I study Whitman, let me have my Lincoln back.'*"

I applauded, and the class followed. "You are now free to converse with old Walt any time you please."

"Good rap," said Betty.

Anita Washington laughed, "Every Wednesday at the Red Star, rap night, starts eight p.m., no cover."

Pens came alive. Some of them were no strangers to the poetry-sports going on around the bars, cash prizes included. That was the same bar where the music was so loud I couldn't hear a word. Wednesdays were for words alone.

My Introduction to Writing Poetry class consisted, I realized, of restless, ironic types like Zed Bennigan, Chloe Chamoix, and Jacob Jason, on the one hand, and mordant, obsessive types like Betty Garland, Matt Borden, and Trudy Helmick. Sylvia Minneaux and Anita Washington fell in between. A reasonably good-humored group.

In the past I had considered dividing my classes into students with ADD (attention deficit disorder) on one side, and people with OCD (obsessive-compulsive disorder) on the other, but while this scheme might have worked generally, it left out the in-between students, often the better students, speaking strictly of assignments. I had once seen a man (not a student) who embodied both types perfectly, and it was he who made me renounce schematizing my charges: he was this guy walking day in and day out on the edge of Highway 65 in Louisiana carrying a big cross on his back, waving at passing cars. That was OCD, like most religions if practiced correctly. Rain or shine, the penitent walked the edge of the highway there, reminding motorists just how far they'd gotten from the Lord, how far they had wandered in the desert. Wandering is ADD, the secular incarnate. This is the perspective from which I viewed my classes: the prayerful on one side, the wanderers on the other. Twixt them stood I, doing now the psychotic rock, now the endless digression. I couldn't get away from this: I am the teacher.

Sylvia Minneaux pointed and read from the blackboard: "We did goatskin notebook for writing down dreams and the Ghost-Companion, but we still didn't do Mont Blanc fountain pen, extra credit if it belonged to Mme Blavatsky, a Chinese coin or a stone in your pocket for rubbing, frequenting places where you can overhear things, tiny recorders, spyglasses, microscopic listening devices, a little man at the back of your head, susceptibility to hypnosis, large sheets of homemade paper, a stack a foot thick, subscription to cable TV. . ."

"That's for next class, we've run out of time now. Don't forget your assignments: an epitogram and familiarizing yourself with your Ghost-Companion. I will add only a small bit of extra homework to what I've already assigned: read a book in the right place."

I told them about how my friend Philip Herter, who was a firm believer in reading the right book in the right place, caused me to read Malcolm Lowry's novel *Under the Volcano* in Mexico. I fell violently in love with it and decided to duplicate some of the Consul's journey from his one moment of happiness in Hotel Francia in Oaxaca all the way through the circles of hell he travels to Death in La Baranca. I intended to stop short of Death, however. I checked in at the Hotel Francia, where the Consul had come out of his alcoholic fog to make love to his beautiful wife and to vow never to drink again. When she falls asleep with a smile on her face, he goes to the bar to have a celebratory beer, then decides to have one mezcal in a nearby bar, then another in a worse bar, and he has a lot of mezcal in circles that take him farther and farther away from his wife and happiness, until he meets Death, the last shot of mezcal. So I had my beer, my first mezcal, my second, many more, and I ended up in a dank dive that displayed nothing but black clay bottles of mezcal on bare shelves. Several sinister gold-toothed guys at a wooden table watched me like alligators waiting for a sick bird to fall into their jaws. A few fat whores dressed in spandex were sitting at another table, looking bored and reading illustrated novels. I knew that I couldn't stand up and that La Baranca might be the next stop, so I motioned one of the women over and said, "Vamos." She was the biggest and meanest of the bunch and she propped me up like a doll out into the street, where I said, "I pay you how much you charge for sex, but you only have to show me the way back to Hotel Francia." She was indignant. "That'll be twice as much!" *No problema.* I got back to the Lowry Happiness Spot and had a three-day hangover that felt like I was upholstered in linoleum inside and the gallons of water I drank just flowed over it without effect.

I said, "In conclusion, yeah, you can read Malcolm Lowry's novel of Mexico in Mexico if you love Death. And read, for the same reason, Thomas Mann's *Death in Venice* in Venice. But since we are not in any of those places, read only local literature by writers who weren't alcoholics. Good luck!"

Everybody, except Trudy Helmick, laughed. Everybody knows that writers are alcoholics. And this was Louisiana. I didn't tell them that *I* was the writer bent on self-destruction, and that *they* were the whores who were supposed to save me. On the other hand, maybe *I* was the whore paid to save *them.* They had their own self-destruction issues, since they had signed up for poetry, and my job, as their leader, was to lead them away from it at the peril of my own life. Otherwise, we might just call the whole thing Introduction to Suicide and get right to it.

"Besides, I am not asking you to read novels—read a book of poetry, it's much shorter, and you can sit under a tree and skip between poems. If you have any questions, e-mail me. Mr. Borden, I have changed my mind. Please don't call your father. It was a ridiculous idea. Giving away these many Ghost-Companions made me realize that graves are superfluous. The whole world is a cemetery, everybody's dead except for the poets. Poets don't need a cemetery."

"They do need milk," Borden said cheerfully, in a tone of voice that made me suspect that he never intended to call his father.

I watched them scamper out, another generation in flight from books. I hadn't even gotten around to discussing their other textbook for the Introduction to Writing Poetry class, namely, *World Poetry of the Stone and Bronze Ages*. The pre-iron chants and stories here were scary and animalistic and I had planned to assign them so that my students could imitate and inhabit the deepest part of their psyches as soon as possible. I *like* to start at the beginning, I adore chronology even though I know only too well (and explain to my advanced classes) that chronology is arbitrary and that you can get to or at anything starting at any point, because all things touch on every other thing with at least one point of their thingness. Or maybe all things are round. Sure, I planned to assign Stone and Bronze Age poetry to inspire students to write a Stone or Bronze Age poem, but I intended to assign also the making of a Stone or Bronze Age weapon, a bronze sword, let's say, or a catapult, or even a slingshot, weapons not meant to be brought to class (only the poem was), but to be useful in the process of being made to the thinking needed to write the poem. I'm not sure what the university or department policy was in the matter of assigning the making of weapons, but I rather suspect that there is something against it. The text-message alert was in place, after all. I hasten to add, just in case one might think those Stone and Bronze poetries simple, that the Homeric stories, the Old Testament, and complex song-and-stories cycles dating from 2500-2000 BCE were written before iron. Everything associated with poetry, including the divine, the erotic, the pastoral, the personal, the humble, the plaint, the lament, and the heroic, were already present before the first iron-tipped arrow entered human flesh.

When they had all gone, I sat in the empty classroom and waited for the familiar wave of futility to wash over me. I checked my e-mail. The first one was from a student:

Professor Codrescu, I'm sorry I had to miss class, I wasn't feeling too good. I went to the infirmary and I have a doctor's note. I realize that I missed the announcement of our assignment due this monday. If you wouldn't mind filling me in I would really appreciate it. Thanks so much for your help, Rebecca Saunders

Hi Rebecca: I assigned everyone a poet to read from the textbook, study, and receive psychic (poetic) advice from for the rest of the semester. The assignment was to write a poem inspired by this Ghost-Companion. Yours is

I stood poised over the keyboard, Sssss, Sssss, Seferis, Solomon (Songs of), Stalin (yes, the young seminarian had written poetry), Samperi (Frank), Sexton (Anne), Sernet (Claude) ... I opened *Poems for the Millennium, Volume Two*, que sera, sera, I closed my eyes and opened them to a blank page between two great ages of poetry, or themes, or ideas (I'm still not sure how this monument is organized), a break maybe between the moderns and the postmoderns, a snow blizzard between the two great wars of the twentieth century, a white cypher, a sphinx.

Yours is the Sphinx. If you hate him, though I don't see how you can, you can trade him in for another poet on

Monday (provided the poet's last name starts with the same letter as yours). And there is also a goatskin notebook, a pen used by a medium, a voice in your head, some spying equipment, and some other parts to this assignment. Ask one of your classmates.

Really. You better get with it, Rebecca, or you won't be ready for the fashion show. I closed the laptop and put it in my backpack. I scooped up Sappho, who protested only slightly, and took her home to Laura.